Ski Magazine's Expert Tips for Better Skiing

SKI MAGAZINE'S

Expert Tips for Better Skiing

BY THE EDITORS OF SKI MAGAZINE

Illustrated

HARPER & ROW, PUBLISHERS
New York, Evanston, San Francisco, London

Portions of this work first appeared in somewhat different form as contributions to *Ski Magazine*.

FIRST EDITION

STANDARD BOOK NUMBER: 06-013921-8

LIBRARY OF CONGRESS CATALOG CARD NUMBER: 72-81372

CONTENTS

1. SKIING BY THE BOOK(S)

Establishment ski teaching is dead—the "establishment" in this case being the way most of us learned to ski, through a systematic progression of stages. What is replacing the highly structured ski teaching and the often rigid results will seem confusing to many skiers who have been taught (or are trying to learn) by the old book. Today or tomorrow, this season or next, you will be faced with several different instruction methods, some amalgamations, and some really individual approaches.

In this section we present the three trend-setting programs that are most popular at ski schools throughout North America. They are: (1) the modified American technique; (2) the Austrian schwups method; (3) the graduated length method (GLM). Actually, all three systems are based on the American technique—that is, they use the American technique maneuvers and sequences when they fit into the learning progressions. The difference is in emphasis: the old American system stresses the idea of perfecting maneuvers such as snowplow and stem turns, while the newer systems touch on these and move quickly on to the real goal—parallel skiing.

The most widespread and uniform of the new teaching systems is the graduated length method, in which skiers start on two-and-a-half or three-foot skis, move on to four-footers, five-footers, and finally to their own skis, all generally within one week of ski instruction. As a rule there are few weekend GLM programs, because people can't learn enough in one or two days of class lessons to ski without an instructor's supervision.

As previously stated, the new Austrian and American methods of learning to ski are very much alike. The former, frequently called the Austrian wide-track system, bypasses, alters, or telescopes several of the snowplow and stem phases of progression of the American technique into a class of turns called *schwups*. But as shown in the following ski learning programs, all three widely used teaching systems reach the desired goal of learning to ski in about the same length of time:

FIRST TWO-HOUR LESSON
(The Big Jump for GLM)

MODIFIED AMERICAN	AUSTRIAN SCHWUPS	GLM	
Straight running	Straight running	Straight running	**Three-foot skis**
Snowplow	Snowplow	Skate from straight run	
Basic snowplow turns	Basic snowplow turns	Turns out of fall line	
		Short and long turns	
		Wide-track turns with hop	
		Use of lift	

First two-hour lesson (left margin label)

SECOND AND THIRD TWO-HOUR LESSONS
(Schwups to Parallel)

MODIFIED AMERICAN	AUSTRIAN SCHWUPS	GLM	
Linked snowplow turns	Linked snowplow turns	Repeat and refine first lesson work	**Three-foot skis**
Traverse	Wide-track Schwups turns out of the fall line		
	Use of the lift		
Stem turns	Linked Schwups turns	Traverse	**Five-foot skis**
Sideslip		Uphill christies	
Uphill christies		Turns out of the fall line	
Stem turns with some sliding at the end		Wide-track linked turns holding poles	
Use of the lift			

Second two-hour lesson / Third two-hour lesson (left margin labels)

FOURTH AND FIFTH TWO-HOUR LESSONS
(American Catches Up)

	MODIFIED AMERICAN	AUSTRIAN SCHWUPS	GLM	
Fourth two-hour lesson	Snowplow christies	Schwups turn garlands	Repeat and review previous lesson	**Five-foot skis**
	Stem christie garland	Stem wedeln	How to ues poles	
	Beginning stem christies			
	Stem christies			
Fifth two-hour lesson	Stem christies with poles	Stem wedeln with poles	Traverse	**Regular-length skis**
	Elementary wide-track parallel turns	Wide-track parallel turns	Uphill christies	
			Parallel turns out of the fall line with poles	
			Wide-track parallel turns	

Skiers taking ski weeks are taught maneuvers in approximately this order. An advantage of the American system is that students can readily transfer from one ski school to another, but proponents of GLM claim that students almost instinctively learn to stem skis for safety during their practice time, which should permit them to attend other ski schools. Those students who practice regularly between lessons and have good coordination should be able to do rudimentary parallel turns with feet apart on an easy slope by the end of the fifth lesson. From this point it is up to the individual to practice and take lessons at regular intervals.

This is where the student who has been following one system can switch to another method for additional help and new ideas. Most students should be doing stem christies with pole action by the fifth lesson in the American system, but much depends on such factors as snow conditions. Many instructors feel that skiers in the East and Midwest are more intense about learning to ski and prefer a systematic, structured approach. Class attitude, they say, is also a factor; enthusiastic groups advance faster in any system.

Straight running (*top*) is taught in all three systems, following the usual maneuvers: learning to carry skis, walking, and simple climbing. The gliding snowplow is taught in both the American and Austrian systems. The new Austrian system stresses simplicity, with fewer exercises and cursory learning of the snowplow turn.

The classic, American-system steered snowplow turn, done slowly and deliberately. In this system there are more structured steps in the learning progression, which means that the student must absorb more theory, but he will also develop a few basic maneuvers to handle difficult terrain and snow.

The key turn of GLM is continuous S-turns on three-foot skis, normally performed during the first day's lesson on very easy slopes by most pupils. Skis of this shortness will swivel easily underfoot with a very small amount of effort, compared to what is needed for six- or seven-foot skis. The parallel turning motion is transferred to longer and longer skis, until the student is on the longest skis he can comfortably handle at his ability.

Linked turns come quickly after the skier learns the basic feeling of schwups: pushing off from one ski to the other and using the legs to make the turn. This can be done quickly and rhythmically even by novices. The biggest problem is that pupils tend to hang on to the steered snowplow turn, which prevents effective schwups.

Most students should be doing stem christies with pole action by the fifth lesson in the American system, but much depends on factors like snow conditions. Many instructors feel that skiers in the East and Midwest are more intense about learning to ski and prefer a systematic, structured approach. Class attitude, they say, is also a factor; enthusiastic groups advance faster in any system. Here you see demonstrator Corky Fowler doing a wide-track stem christie in which the outside ski steers the turn, and the skis are brought together parallel after the change of direction has been started.

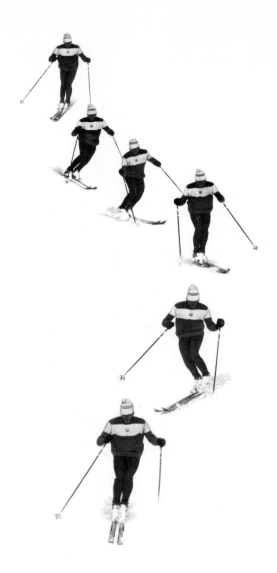

Using regular-length skis, the GLM student learns to ski down the fall line and turn up into the hill. Now instead of just "wiggling" the skis around as he did with the three-footers, he must slide them in a smooth arc. Throughout, the emphasis is to use the legs to turn the skis, and gradually the student builds up through the ski week to this technique refinement.

2. SKIING FOR BEGINNERS

In the company of experienced skiers, the beginner may feel somewhat less than heroic. Yet, as he moves from one maneuver to the next and becomes master of his skis, no temporary feeling of inferiority can squelch his sense of accomplishment. The first no-fall downhill run with snowplow turns can be as thrilling to him as a smooth series of parallel turns to the advanced skier.

Today, ski learning is divided into three stages: basic, advanced, and racing. The basic technique—which is divided into beginner, intermediate, and expert classes—is instruction from the beginning stages through parallel, short-swing, and other "expert" turns. The advanced technique teaches better parallel skiers to ski all snow conditions and types of slopes with finesse and control. The racing technique is intended for those few who are in prime physical condition and can apply the refinements necessary for competition skiing.

One of the achievements of modern skiing, as described in Chapter 1, is the way it has reduced and simplified the learning process to an absolute minimum. But what remains is important and stays important, even if the skier should reach international racing ranks, for even the best skiers have occasion to use the very basics, such as a snowplow stop or turn. Here are some tips from our experts to help the beginner improve his skiing.

The Correct Natural Stance

by GLENN T. KIEDAISCH
Certified, U.S. Eastern Amateur Ski Association

A beginner should try to develop a natural, well-balanced stance over his skis, one that requires only a minimum effort to maintain. To achieve a good stance, stand on level terrain with skis parallel and several inches apart. First, lean forward to create ankle pressure against the front of your boots, as the "ghost" in the illustration is doing. Then bend at the knees, bringing your hips and upper body back over the center of your skis while maintaining light pressure against the front part of your boots (main figure). Try this relaxed body position in several short runs downhill over easy terrain, using your legs to absorb bumps in the terrain.

Bending only at the knees often increases muscle tension by placing the body in a position that is difficult to maintain—ankles straight and thighs horizontal. On the other hand, exaggerated forward ankle bend also makes balance and a relaxed position difficult to attain.

How to Climb with Ease

by ROBERT SCHARFF

The herringbone is the quickest means of walking straight up a hill. The skis are formed into a V, with the tails of the skis forming the point of the V, and are then put on the inside edges. Weight is shifted to one ski, and a backslip is prevented by bracing against the opposite pole. The unweighted ski is then moved forward and the process repeated.

In the herringbone, the points of the poles should not be ahead of the skier's boots. If the poles are too far forward, particularly on steeper hills, they will have to be rearranged before the next stride is taken. This breaks the rhythm of the "herringbone" stride.

Pick Up That Tip!

by JACKIE STEINMANN
Certified, Far West Ski Instructors' Association

Another method of climbing a hill is by sidestepping. But in sidestepping up a hill—particularly in deep or wet snow—many beginners experience difficulty because they don't sidestep the whole uphill ski at once. Rather, they forget and allow the tip to drag in the snow. I often tell students to feel their toes press on the top of the inside of the boot as they lift the ski off the ground. This will automatically cause the whole ski to be lifted off the snow and will get the ankle and lower leg into the correct position for sidestepping. Other tips to remember: Use relatively small steps, and get a good platform on one ski before picking up the other.

Look Up to Step Turn

by RÉAL CHARETTE
Certified, Canadian Ski Instructors' Alliance

A slope with even a very mild slant can pose hazards for beginners who
want to turn around while climbing uphill. Instead of the difficult kick
turn or the normal turn facing downhill, try this one facing uphill. Put
your hands on top of the pole grips for support and plant your uphill pole
in the snow slightly behind your skis. Now step around the uphill pole,
opening the tips of the skis into a herringbone position as you turn to
face up the hill. The important point is not to remove the uphill pole (the
right pole in the illustration above) as you step around, but do remove
the downhill pole at each step and use it for momentary support and
balance.

The Key for Kick Turns

by DAVE YOUMANS
Certified, Rocky Mountain Ski Instructors' Association

Until a beginning skier develops his "ski legs," he may find it difficult to lift and twist the entire weight of his ski in a kick turn. To make turns easier, try the following method. Place both skis at a right angle to the fall line and plant both poles in the snow behind you, as illustrated on the opposite page. Swing the downhill ski back and forth several times. Let it gain momentum, then make a full-swing, football-like kick—fully extending your leg until the ski tail stands in the snow next to the tip of the opposite ski. Then turn the upright ski backward before letting it fall parallel to the uphill ski. Transfer your weight to the downhill ski before swinging the other ski around.

Get a Good Grip on Your Pole

by RUSS RANKIN
Certified, U.S. Eastern Amateur Ski Association

Many skiers use an orchestra director's grip on their poles, with the thumb and only one or two fingers. Although the pole swings easily because of the loose grip, a strong pole plant is not possible.

Grasp each pole firmly, wrapping all five fingers around the grip. Point the knuckles straight ahead and draw the pole plant. You'll find that a firm grip will help you begin each turn from a strong position.

Heave-Ho and Get Up

by JANET NELSON
Certified, Canadian Ski Instructors' Alliance

Even after learning the standard technique for getting up, skiers still have trouble making those last couple of inches needed to get upright. So, here's a way of helping you to overcome gravity by bringing those big leg muscles into play. First, arrange your body with skis downhill and pointed across the slope. Second, pull your knees up to your chest. Third, put the pole tips in the snow next to your hip. Put one hand over the pole baskets and the other over the pole handles. Now, rock back a bit and then forcefully throw your upper body forward toward the ski tips. Do this in rhythmic stages: *Heave!* (lean back), *Ho!* (forward), and *Hup!* (get up). The last step requires a normal amount of push from the lower hand and pull from the upper hand. Once your upper body is slightly up off the snow, it will give your legs room to work, and up you come!

Hands Forward Like Headlights

by Tom Moore

Certified, Canadian Ski Instructors' Alliance

A novice skier often reveals his fear of skiing when he trys to stop in a snowplow. Drawing his arms and hands in close to his body, he turns his wrists inward, and both poles jut awkwardly out to either side. This "fear position" (*A*) actually increases a skier's difficulty in controlling his skis because his body becomes tense and rigid.

Imagine you are skiing at night, and think of the grips of your ski poles as headlights (*B*). Point them downhill in the direction of your descent. To be effective, your headlights must point straight ahead to light your way, not upward or inward. If you keep your hands ahead of your body in a waist-high position, you'll soon develop a relaxed, stable body position for better control in all ski maneuvers.

B

Forward to Fan the Tails

by KYLE CORNELIUS
Certified, U.S. Eastern Amateur Ski Association

Actually, the greatest confidence-builder in skiing is the snowplow, because it provides the skier's first experience in being able to control the skis. In assuming the snowplow position, however, many beginners have difficulty pushing the tails of their skis out into the fan or "V" position while sliding downhill. Some catch the outside edges; some find the tips separating too much; others push one ski out, but not the other.

The solution to these problems is to lean forward at the ankles, and to keep the knees pushing forward toward the tips of the skis. In this way, the tails become unweighted, and thus slide easily when the heels are pushed outward. There are other benefits, too: weight forward will prevent the tips from crossing, and the beginner starts at an early stage to learn the "forward lean" habit.

Power-Brake to Stop Your Snowplow

by RUEDI WYRSCH
Certified, Swiss National Ski School and U.S. Eastern Amateur Ski Association

To feel confident on a crowded slope, it's important to know how to stop quickly. However, many beginners have difficulty snowplowing to a complete stop.

Here's how to get additional power. Just before a snowplow stop, raise your hands to shoulder height. Then, suddenly lower your hands down to your knees while using your leg muscles to push out the tails of your skis. Dropping your arms will exert downward pressure on the inside edges of your skis to stop their forward motion. Using your arms for extra power, you'll soon gain complete control over your skis in a snowplow.

Pole Power

by JIM BENSON
Certified, Canadian Ski Instructors' Alliance

Ski tyros are frequently insensitive to their own maneuvers on skis. A skier may think that both legs are flexed equally in a snowplow when, in fact, he is flexing one leg while stiffening the other.

If you experience difficulty in a snowplow, try the following exercise. Start a snowplow on gentle terrain and remove both pole straps from your wrists. Place the pole shafts directly behind your knees and press forward evenly on both ends of the shafts. Then start downhill in a straight snowplow. You will be forced to assume a good low position over your skis. Equal pressure on the end of the pole shafts will cause your legs to bend evenly to weight both skis. Be sure to apply constant pressure against the snow with both feet to keep your skis in a wide V. As an aid to turning in a snowplow, simply push harder on one side of the pole shafts to force more weight to the outside ski of the turn.

24

Sneak into a Snowplow

by LARRY TROXELL
Certified, Rocky Mountain Ski Instructors' Association

If you've mastered the art of straight downhill running and the thought of spreading your skis in a snowplow still frightens you, relax! Find a gentle slope and try this snowplow exercise. Start from a straight downhill running position with skis parallel and several inches apart. As you begin to slide downhill, lift the tail of one ski a few inches off the ground for one second. Set it back down on the snow, then lift the other ski. When you have tried this exercise several times, add a slight push with your heel each time you put your ski on the snow.

After repeating this exercise several times, you'll learn to relax and to spread your ski tails into a smooth, controlled snowplow.

Stop Your Tips from Crossing

by DIXI NOHL
Certified, Austrian Association of Professional Ski Instructors and U.S.
   Eastern Amateur Ski Association

Beginning skiers often attempt to make a snowplow turn by twisting their bodies in the direction of the turn and by pushing the turning ski ahead in an attempt to make it come around. One frequent result is that weight goes onto the inside ski and the tips cross.

The secret of the snowplow turn is not to think of turning the skis. Instead, concentrate on getting your body weight transferred onto the outside ski of the turn. A ski is designed with curved sides (called *side camber*), and once you've applied your body weight forward over the ski and put it on its edge, it will virtually turn for you. So work to put weight on the turning ski and the ski will turn without further thought or effort on your part.

26

Watch Your Shoulder Dip

by Art Milman
Certified, Rocky Mountain Ski Instructors' Association

In their eagerness to do the snowplow turn effectively, some skiers overdo the dropping or "dipping" of the outside shoulder, arm, and hand at the end of a turn. This results in a stiff inside leg and can lead to other faults, such as dragging the ski pole in the snow and allowing the weight to move back on the skis.

The problem may be that you can't see how much you are dipping your shoulder. To get a graphic picture of this, hold your poles, in both hands, horizontally across your body. Practice the shoulder dip while standing still and try not to move your arms. Then, do the same thing in a snowplow turn. As you draw your outside shoulder back, you can watch your shoulder dip. Furthermore, you can visually control this motion by adjusting the position of your poles. The poles should be approximately parallel to the incline of the hill.

Fingertip Control

Certified, Rocky Mountain Ski Instructors' Association

Beginners learning to snowplow often try to force their skis around turns by swinging their hips downhill. A skier who rotates his hips in a snowplow turn will finish facing uphill and in a very awkward position to begin a new turn (*A*).

To correct this common fault, try an easy exercise. Place your fingertips at waist level and bend sideways at the waist over your fingers to start each turn (*B*). In this position you'll feel your hips turning against your hands if rotation occurs and your fingertips will serve to discourage swinging your hips in the direction of the turn. After a little practice you'll discover that bending the upper body sideways, in combination with increased knee and ankle pressure on the outside ski, allows you to finish each snowplow turn facing downhill and in a good position to make a new turn.

A

B

Use a Wide V for Snowplow Turns

by RONALD H. LEVINE
Certified, Canadian Ski Instructors' Alliance

Trying to weight one ski in a snowplow turn, a skier often catches an outside edge and loses his balance. This situation occurs frequently when a beginner uses a narrow snowplow and transfers his weight improperly to the outside edge of his turning ski.

Using a wide enough snowplow, you'll find you can transfer your weight smoothly to the inside edge of the turning ski. To measure the correct width for your snowplow, arrange your skis in a V on flat terrain. Transfer your weight from one ski to the other. Increase the size of your snowplow until you're sure there's no weight on the outside edges of your skis. Then try a snowplow of equal size on a gradual slope, maintaining your wide V while turning.

Watch the Weighted Ski

by CHARLES McDONALD, JR.
Certified, Rocky Mountain Ski Instructors' Association

As a last resort, beginners often try to steer snowplow turns with their shoulders. Unfortunately, upper body rotation in the direction of a turn usually results in an unstable body position, with the skier's weight transferred to the wrong ski.

Here's a simple cure for this common fault. Starting from a straight snowplow, turn your head and shoulders toward the tail of the outside, or turning, ski. Fix your eyes on the portion of the ski behind your heel until you complete one turn. Practice turns in both directions until you curb any inclination to rotate your shoulders. Besides halting upper body angulation, you'll learn to rely on your ankles, knees, and hips for power to turn your skis.

Tip That Hip!

by RON NICCOLI
Certified, Pacific Northwest Ski Instructors' Association

Actually, angulation is used in all ski maneuvers from snowplow turns to wedeln to give edging power to the skis. You can see this position most readily in the traverse: the lateral plane of the hips is tipped down the slope about parallel with the fall line of the slope. Holding this position causes the knees to move into the hill, thus edging the skis, at the same time that the upper body leans down the slope. The uphill ski, knee, hip, and shoulder are advanced slightly. You won't be wrong in angulation if you keep the angle of your hips on the same plane as the slope.

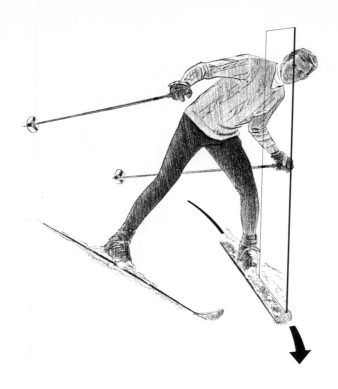

Peek-A-Boo Turn

by RAINER MOBERG
Certified, Canadian Ski Instructors' Alliance

Beginning skiers often have trouble moving the upper parts of their bodies toward the outside of a turn. In fact, skiers who forget to hold this outward-leaning stance when they are learning their first stem turns have a problem. Without it, the hips tend to move out over the turning or stemmed ski. Instead of carving the turn, the ski goes flat on the snow and the turn cannot be continued.

To correct this fault, imagine that the weighted or turning ski has a thin, solid wall higher than your head and extending down the middle of your ski from boot to tip. As you stem your uphill ski and shift your weight onto it, try to peek around the corner of the wall in the direction you're turning. Keep peeking all the way through the turn. This peek-a-boo position will keep your weight over the turning ski and you will be able to carve the turn.

34

Tip to Turn

by ALBERT BOLOWIEC, JR.
Certified, U.S. Eastern Amateur Ski Association

In a ski turn, the forces generated by the turning of the legs require a countering force in the upper body for the skier to stay balanced. The trick is to learn and get accustomed to this position of leaning out in a ski turn. One way to learn it is by doing linked snowplow turns through a series of poles planted down the fall line. Start down the hill in a snowplow position with both arms raised about 45 degrees from your sides. As you reach a pole, raise the arm nearest it and reach for your heel with the other arm. Repeat at each pole. You'll automatically find your upper body tipping to the outside of the turn and transferring your weight to the edge of the turning ski, where it belongs.

Roll the Inside Ankle

by CHUCK CASWELL
Certified, U.S. Eastern Amateur Ski Association

In heavy spring snow, the snowplow turn is difficult enough, but many skiers tend to make it even more tiring by using improper edging. If you find your snowplows seem to be strenuous, you may be fighting the turn with the inside edge of your unweighted ski. Try rolling the ankle of the inside ski slightly out, away from the weighted turning ski. You'll find that snowplow turns can be fun even in the slush of spring.

No-Pole Turns

by MURDO MACDONALD, M.D.

Even though beginners should be encouraged to use the poles to help them turn, inevitably there comes a point when the skier has to stop for a bit and concentrate on eliminating the pole habits that form unconsciously, the habits of overuse. Even the advanced skier typically thrusts his pole too hard and typically leans on the pole as he swings around a turn (instead of using a light pole plant to trigger the turn). Then there is the skier who uses the pole as a crutch, dragging it in the snow or jabbing away at the snow as he goes through the turn.

There is a way to test whether you are overthrusting, leaning, dragging, or jabbing. Make a few turns on easy terrain without using your poles at all; this will quickly show up any errors in pole overuse, and will demonstrate both whether you are using your legs properly to supply the lift for a parallel turn and whether you are staying on the outside ski during a stem turn. A few runs will help you to stay on top of your skis, improve your balance, and make you realize that a good skier can easily ski without poles, and that he uses his poles sparingly on normal terrain.

Snowplow Turn Savvy

by JUNIOR BOUNOUS

Certified, Intermountain Ski Instructors' Association

To summarize the techniques of making the snowplow turn easily, there are three factors to keep in mind: (1) even edging—putting both skis up on edge equally; (2) emphatic weight shift—leaning well over the outside ski of the turn; (3) proper width—keeping a greater spread between the tails than between the tips. Uneven edging, lack of weight shift and lack of proper width at the tails will lead to slow, agonizing, difficult turns.

In the illustration on the opposite page, the skier in the picture starts out (*top left*) with ski tips a little too far apart and with too little weight on the turning ski. By the middle picture, these minor faults have become major ones. The tips are almost as far apart as the tails. The skier has raised her outside arm, trying to twist her way through the turn, and no wonder—her faults have made it impossible to turn properly. Her arm movement takes even more weight off her turning ski, so her turn slows down even more than before. In the last picture, she's made it around, but she's put so much into it that she's exhausted. On the right-hand side of the page, I show a tips-together, tails-apart, easy skiing position right from the beginning. The skier doesn't attempt to twist through the turn, but leans well over the outside ski: the skis then go around easily, without any extraordinary expenditure of energy on his part. I can ski like this all day, without having to take a deep breath.

A

Hold the Hip Back

by DIXI NOHL

Certified, Austrian Association of Professional Ski Instructors and U.S. Eastern Amateur Ski Association

In teaching the traverse, I often hear would-be instructors giving their friends the following advice: "Keep your shoulder back; reverse your shoulder; face down the hill. . . ." What often results is the awkward position shown in *A* in the illustration. Note that although the downhill shoulder is pulled back, the hip is jutting forward and down the slope, blocking angulation and making it almost impossible for the skier to hold his feet together. If you want to correct your traverse, practice holding your downhill hip back and into the hill. If you can learn to hold your hip back, the rest of your body, including your shoulders, will normally fall into a good position for traversing (*B*). Too much emphasis on shoulders, too little on the hip, can result in a faulty body position.

40

B

41

Be a "Penny Pincher"

by MARY-CLAIRE DEMELBAUER
Certified, U.S. Eastern Amateur Ski Association

If you want to save on spills and spend more time skiing, here's a tip to speed you on your way to the top of the mountain. Avoid the natural inclination to lean forward or uphill in a traverse. Learn to be a penny pincher!

Imagine a penny pinched between your downhill hip and ribs. By tipping your upper body toward the bottom of the hill to hold the penny in place, you'll learn edge control and correct weight distribution for more advanced ski maneuvers. If you lean forward or uphill, you'll lose your correct position—and the penny!

42

The "Leaning Tower"

by JOAN KURISKO
Certified, Canadian Ski Instructors' Alliance

A correct traverse is similar to a tower of children's building blocks, in which, if one block is out of line, the balance of the tower must be restored by placing the next block on the other side. In a traverse a skier's knees are pressed into the hill to compensate for the slope of the hill. Then the upper body leans downhill to compensate for the imbalance caused by pushing the knees uphill.

On a steep slope, press your knees strongly into the hill to hold a straight traverse; lean your upper body out to counteract the knee action. On a gentle slope avoid the extreme position; use only enough knee pressure to edge the skis in a straight traverse.

Raise the Uphill Shoulder

by Ruedi Wyrsch

Certified, Swiss National Ski School and U.S. Eastern Amateur Ski Association

To grasp the importance of shoulder position, stand in a traverse position and lower the uphill shoulder (*A*). This position, which is common among skiers especially where icy conditions exist, encourages skis to flatten against the slope and creates uncontrollable sideways slipping.

Now raise the uphill shoulder; feel your skis automatically shift onto their uphill edges (*B*).

Next, apply what you've learned about shoulder position to your turns. During the completion phase of each turn, raise the uphill shoulder; you'll improve edge bite for the next traverse.

Body Hinges

by CORKY FOWLER

Remember the expression "bend the knees"? As a result of this often repeated advice, many skiers fall into the habit of bending the knees only, merely moving the body weight up and down.

Gain greater flexibility and better balance by learning to use three body hinges—ankles, knees, and hips—while skiing. Initiate forward movement first in the ankles, second in the knees, and third in the hips. Move the body weight forward and aft as well as up and down. Make use of all available balancing aids to handle your skis on varied terrain.

A

Side by Side, the Knees Shall Ride

by Dixi Nohl
Certified, Austrian Association of Professional Ski Instructors and U.S. Eastern Amateur Ski Association

Skiers who try to keep their skis rigidly together often develop a habit of tucking one knee behind the other in a traverse (*A*). Although this may help keep the skis together, tucking one knee behind the other impairs a skier's balance and ability to edge his skis properly.

If you stand in a traverse with one knee tucked behind the other, you will notice that even a slight push will cause a loss of balance. Next, try rolling both knees into and then away from the hill, and note the limited mobility of your knees when one knee is tucked behind the other. To improve your position, move the downhill knee forward so that your knees are side by side and your body position is stable over both skis, to remain well balanced despite irregular terrain. Again, press your knees in and away from the hill (*B*). Notice how easy it is to move your knees laterally in this position as compared to your former stance.

46

B

Hip Checkup

by Jim Lucas

Certified, Pacific Northwest Ski Instructors' Association

An easy way to check to see if your hips are properly positioned in a traverse is to glance down at the back of your downhill boot. If you can see your heel while skiing across a hill (*A*), your entire body is likely to be in a good position. If you cannot see your heel (*B*), it is because your lower hip is twisted forward out of proper alignment with the rest of your body. In a traverse the uphill side of your body should lead slightly, so your hips are square to your line of travel. With your body in a natural, balanced position, and with ankles and knees flexed, you can easily turn your knees up into the slope to control the edges of your skis. In this position you can glance down at your heel without twisting or distorting your stance. Use this quick visual check often to develop a strong traverse position.

B

A

Step Up to a Traverse Position

by BARBARA MURDOCK

If you're just learning to traverse and have difficulty remembering the proper body position, the following tip may help relieve some of your confusion.

Point both skis straight across the fall line with one pole in the snow next to your downhill ski boot. Reach uphill so that your arm is straight, and keep the other pole planted in the snow. Then sidestep uphill until you reach the uphill ski pole basket. At this point, your upper body is bent sideways toward the lower ski pole. Assuming good forward flex at the ankles and knees, you are set in just the right position for a good traverse.

After you've tried this exercise, it's important that you learn to feel natural with your upper body bent out, toward the bottom of the hill, so that you start to use upper body angulation in all of your traverses.

51

Step Up for Confidence

by L. D. LOMEN
Associate Certified Instructor, Far West Ski Instructors' Association

Novice skiers practicing a traverse often look stiff enough to be blown over by a light breeze. A good way to build confidence for the skier who is just learning to cross a hill with feet together is to start a shallow traverse and step uphill with the tip of the uphill ski. Then, when the ski is securely in the snow, put your weight onto the uphill edge and pull the downhill ski up next to it. Make several steps uphill from the traverse until your skis come to a complete stop. For best results, keep the size of the steps fairly small. Practice this maneuver in both directions; also, vary the steepness of the traverse and the speed of the steps. This maneuver is both easy and fun, particularly in soft snow, and helps build confidence and relaxed skiing.

52

Easy One-Two Traverse

by Corky Fowler

On an intermediate slope, practice using only enough edge to prevent your skis from slipping sideways: this is the object of any traverse. Balance your body weight over the skis until you feel solid—simply stand on your edges. The key lies in your ability to place your skis on edge with a subtle sideways motion of the knees and ankles.

You should be able to traverse across even a steep hill in a very relaxed position, leaving behind only two very narrow tracks.

53

Close the Scissors

by PAUL PFOSI

Certified, Swiss National Ski School and U.S. Eastern Amateur Ski Association

In traversing, many skiers have a tendency to get the uphill ski too far ahead of the downhill ski, opening their legs in a scissor position. This causes a whole chain of mistakes: the skier tends to sit back, putting his weight on the ski tails, compensating for this by bending over at the waist in order to get some weight forward. His comma position is nonexistent, his downhill ski is flat, and he may lock one knee behind the other.

It is a hard fault to correct, so it is wise to work on it when it fi st shows up. One exercise that helps is to ski directly down the fall line of a very gentle slope, keeping your ski tips exactly even. You may separate your feet a little for balance. Then, when you traverse again, concentrate on keeping your ski tips even (again, you may have your feet separated slightly) and your weight well forward on your skis. You'll find that your body position and your stability are greatly improved when you have closed the scissors.

A

Slip the Tips

B

by JUNIOR BOUNOUS
Certified, Intermountain Ski Instructors' Association

Most beginners experience difficulty learning to sideslip because ski tips separate frequently and the tails often cross. To gain control over your skis in a sideslip, learn to control the tips of your skis, then the tails, in the following exercise.

From a traverse, step the upper ski tip uphill several feet and draw the lower ski up parallel so that the skis are perpendicular to the fall line. Then push your knees and feet toward the bottom of the hill, as illustrated left, to flatten the ski tips. Keep your legs flexed and your weight slightly forward while facing downhill to hold the tips together as they slide down to your original traverse (diagram *A*). Re-edge the skis to prevent further slipping by pressing your knees back in toward the hill. Practice this maneuver again: step the tips uphill; then edge, slide, and re-edge (diagram *B*). Ski poles may be planted in the snow for additional balance during the exercise. When you've learned to control the ski tips in a sideslip, try the same exercise but center your weight slightly farther back to make the tails slide.

55

A   B

Keeping the Feet Together in Traverse

by BILLY KIDD

If you can't keep your feet together in a traverse, you are probably leaning uphill with your downhill shoulder in a higher position than your uphill shoulder (*A*). When you fall, you fall uphill. It's very hard for many skiers to lean downhill, but if you press your knees into the hill to make a steady base and drop your downhill hand and shoulder (*B*), you'll establish a better position. Then, if your skis start sliding downhill, your upper body can move along over your skis in a balanced position.

Ban the Backward Slide

by BILL BRIGGS

Certified, U.S. Eastern Amateur Ski Association, Far West Ski Instructors'
  Association, Intermountain Ski Instructors' Association

Beginners who are just learning how to sideslip often are bothered by
the fear of sliding backward across the hill. It isn't always easy to keep
your skis at right angles to the hill to prevent a backward slide, but there
is a perfectly easy way to stop yourself if your skis do start to slide backward. Lift your downhill ski and place the front of it across the hill. It
will quickly brake you to a stop.

This is an easy maneuver to perform and a useful addition to any
skier's repertoire.

Unweighting for Beginners

by OTHMAR SCHNEIDER

The following are the two basic ways for beginners to learn unweighting:

Run and hop

Run and Hop

This is the first unweighting that new skiers do, but it is equally useful for more advanced skiers who are having trouble getting weight off both skis at once. Simply bend down and hop up, lifting the tails of the skis. Begin by maintaining a wide stance, with feet separated about six inches, and do the hopping first on a flat spot without moving forward, then advance to a gentle slope at a slow speed. When you become more secure and coordinated, you can gradually move your feet closer together.

Edge Sensitivity

The snowplow skier learns to stop by edging his skis and pushing out on the tails. A slightly more advanced stop is executed by starting in a straight running position with body bent low over the skis. From this

58

position, hop up (this unweights the skis) and push the tails out into a snowplow. To get the feel of this up-unweighting, practice this first on a flat spot without forward momentum.

This kind of stop can also be done with down-unweighting. Start with a high stance in a straight running position, then quickly sink down and push your ski tails out. For an instant your weight on the skis will be reduced, enabling you to push the tails out. This kind of unweighting takes acute timing and coordination, but it produces more precise movements. Try it and you'll get a keen sense of what your skis' edges can do to help you control your speed.

Edge sensitivity

Unweighting with Feeling

by PETER PALMER
Certified, U.S. Eastern Amateur Ski Association

The greatest single reason skiers fall backwards is that instead of rising up and forward to unweight their skis, they stand straight up, failing to keep up with the acceleration of their skis. Because ski terrain is sloped downhill, unweighting requires an up and forward motion off the balls of the feet. To unweight while keeping a balanced position over the skis, concentrate on feeling weight on the balls of your feet when you rise up to unweight and again when you sink down to complete the turn. With practice you'll be making turns executed with up-forward unweighting.

Off the Fall Line for Beginners

by Dixi Nohl

Certified, Austrian Association of Professional Ski Instructors and U.S. Eastern Amateur Ski Association

The difficulty in skiing a slope that slants off the fall line (that is, slants in one direction only) is that you must prolong your turn in one direction, while shortening it in another. It becomes boring and tiring to traverse or turn one way for an extended period. You think the slope will never end.

Actually, slanted or off-the-fall-line slopes need not be difficult or boring. You can combine a number of different fast and slow maneuvers on these slopes to make them an interesting challenge. Here are two techniques for beginners when skiing off the fall line:

The open-stance sideslip

Open Stance Sideslip

One advantage of an off-the-fall-line slope is that it is an ideal place to perfect the forward sideslip. With the ski tips pointed up into the slope, place your feet six to eight inches apart, with the uphill ski about

61

a boot length ahead. Now place your pole baskets uphill behind your body and push yourself off as you bend your knees and ankles. Let your skis slide down and forward at the same angle of drift as the slope.

Merengue Snowplow

Start down the fall line of a slanted slope in an ordinary snowplow position—feet wide apart, tips close, tails separated—but as your skis begin to move, bend your lower knee immediately and edge that ski slightly. This will slow your speed and also turn the skis into the slope. Just before you come to a complete halt, stand up by straightening your knees; this will let the skis drift down the slanted slope again. When you gain momentum, bend that lower knee again and keep repeating this combination of maneuvers—the effect is something like doing the merengue.

3. TIPS FOR WOMEN SKIERS

"If a lady comes to my class, the first thing I tell her is she has good-looking stretch pants, even if she doesn't have a nice-type shape. If she makes a lousy turn, I don't tell her she makes a lousy turn. I tell her it's not a bad turn, you know, cute. You have to please them by smiling a lot." Mario Podorieszach, ski school director at Mont Orford, Quebec, and a charming guy from a lady's point of view, made these remarks, not to belittle his female students, but because he feels this approach pacifies them; they have fun in class, and some may even learn to ski a little. This condescending attitude among ski teachers is not atypical, and worse, it is accepted by the women students, who leave the classes with a hopelessly inelegant, graceless, timid style of skiing—on the bunny slopes.

Everyone knows that men ski for sport and women ski to be with men. Besides, women are different. What man could ski with the anatomical hang-ups that women are plagued with:

1. Broad, tilted hips
2. Shorter legs
3. Half the muscle mass
4. Lower center of gravity
5. Smaller heart and lungs
6. Looser knee and hip joints
7. Lower metabolic rate
8. Difficulty maintaining body heat

Besides these biological differences, there are the weird psychological problems (whatever their cause—innate, environmental, glandular or astrological) that are allegedly peculiar to females: lack of self-confidence, sensitivity to criticism, proneness to accidents, easy discouragement, hostility toward good-natured kidding, lack of aggression, poor competitive spirit and general emotional instability. Face it—ski technique was developed by men, for the male anatomy and mentality; with all their inborn limitations, you can't expect more from women. Or can you?

Some women do ski very well, and a few have adapted to ski technique so well that they can outclass most men on a race course. Many instructors claim that women learn the early stages of skiing faster and easier than men do simply because they listen and try harder, rather than relying on brute force.

We at *Ski Magazine* challenged the theory of the female skier's natural inferiority and asked some top ski instructors (all men) of the Canadian Ski Instructors' Alliance why most females ski poorly, even after a promising start and tender-loving-care instruction. The teachers themselves accept a good share of the responsibility. "I believe we can blame most of it on the teacher," says Wayne Bradford, former assistant director of the CSIA instructor certification program, "and I don't think we've thought enough about the problems. We generally just try to teach women as we do men, and we don't think of structural differences."

Women face their worst learning problem, say the instructors, just standing on skis; they are stiff-legged, leaners-into-the-hill. That is, women are actually doing the most natural thing: leaning uphill away from the steep slope and standing straight. The instructor right away is fighting her instinct for self-preservation. In addition, most women just aren't strong enough, or don't think they are, to turn a pair of skis. Remember that to maintain a constant speed and control on the fall line of a steep slope, you have to flail those skis from one side to the other, and that's where you really notice the difference. It's not just women who can't do that, of course. Lots of men, too, are out of shape. Oddly enough, in specifying the skiing errors of women, the instructors found that many of these are typical of male skiers as well.

"Most skiers are tail pushers. They turn by making a jerking movement, then a sideslip, a jerk, and a sideslip. This tail pushing is just extranatural for a girl, because she doesn't have as much strength in her legs, and yet she has more weight around her hips," says Karl Jost, former director of the instructor certification courses for CSIA. "In other words, a girl uses her hips as a source of power by throwing them to one side or the other to get the skis started in a turn. Women don't use their upper bodies much, either. They often look very reversed. What's above and below the hips seems to play very little role in their turns. A skier can carve a turn only when he or she is up, out and forward, with the upper body at about the same angle as the shins."

That "angle of the shins" is another problem common to women, and compounds the problem of getting the upper body forward. The instruction to "bend forward" is often interpreted as bending at the waist instead of in the ankles, and this results in the rear end sticking out. "Women just don't like to stick their chins out," says Bill Williams, a CSIA examiner. "A man is not as afraid to lean a little bit forward." The instructors feel that more emphasis on forward position and ankle bending at earlier stages in skiing might help women overcome this inhibition or fear of forward lean.

There is one classic position on skis that—pants, padded parkas, and long hair notwithstanding—really separates the girls from the boys: the knock-kneed tripod. Women resort to this stance when looking for extra strength or support, the theory being that the muscles of two legs are better than one. The result not only looks ungainly, but also puts too much weight on the uphill ski. The remedy is to use a wide-track stance with the knees and feet about equally separated, until legs are stronger and balance is improved.

Apparently the cause of this tripod position is the female anatomy. According to Georges Joubert and Jean Vuarnet, authors of *How to Ski the New French Way,* a woman's knee and hip joints are not as firm and rigid as a man's. Not only does this make it easy to assume a tripod stance, but it may be the basis for much female inelegance on skis. Because of this so-called articular looseness, women cannot edge their skis easily. In order to get a secure stance, they resort to a muscular blockage of the hips (the tail-pushing position that Karl Jost spoke of), but from this position they cannot make rapid leg movements to turn the skis. Women racers overcome their looser knee and hip joints by angulating during a turn more than their male teammates have to do.

How about the women who do ski very well? Apparently, they have by instinct adapted certain nuances of technique that help them to compensate for physiological weaknesses. The next step is for ski instructors to experiment with teaching ideas and exercises and to alter the system, where necessary, for women. Still, one major obstacle remains: even the most inspired and enthusiastic teacher can't overcome the lack of motivation noticeable in many women who don skis. For those women who really do want to learn, however, and for the instructors who really want to teach them, there may be some comfort in a recent study conducted at Michigan State University on the attitudes of female athletes: "The ambition of a woman climbs higher than that of a man, and there is no doubt as to the fact that a woman's will to learn and to attain can cause her, under a good teacher, to reach heights far beyond her innate talents."

Our poll of instructors, male and female, yielded some ideas on how women can learn to ski better:

1. Get the feeling of being up and forward—think "up."

2. Reach out with both poles when making turns to keep your hips out of the action.

3. Take lessons from a woman—you'll learn faster, because she understands your problems as if they were her own.

4. Angulate more, more, more—particularly when you go to plant your pole.

5. Never take a class with your husband; you may hold back in order not to show him up, or you may show him up and ski alone next season.

6. For parallel skiing, think feet together, rather than legs or knees together.

7. Do sit-ups every day to strengthen those stomach muscles.

8. Get a parka big enough to allow you to move your arms. Most women instructors buy them one size larger than their normal clothes.

9. Have your bindings mounted slightly forward (one-fourth to one-half inch) of the normal position.

10. Force yourself to lean away from the hill, point your head downhill.

11. If your instructor doesn't turn you on, get a new one.

12. Keep your upper body moving; don't let it get hung up behind your feet.

13. Use lighter skis and poles and comfortable boots.

14. Anticipate where you are going, and don't look at your boots or skis.

15. Don't take lessons from a boy friend or husband.

Greater angulation is one of the keys to better skiing for women. As Christa Worle and Othmar Schneider ski the same slope, she must tilt her upper body much more to get her edges to bite. Angulation requires a psychological conquest; it takes courage to lean away from the hill.

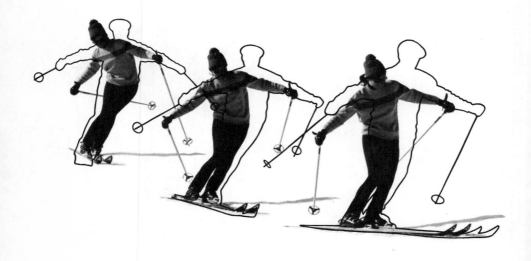

Three errors common among women skiers are not enough forward ankle bend, legs forming a tripod position (here one knee is tucked behind the other to lock the tripod) and too much reverse in the upper body. The overlay shows Othmar Schneider making the same turn, ankles well bent, legs firm, upper body forward and moving with the turn.

Using wide stance and keeping almost the same amount of space between the knees as between the feet, can help break the knock-kneed, tripod habit. When legs are stronger and balance has improved, feet can be moved closer together.

Bending the ankles, angulating, and skiing with the upper body well forward, a girl can carve a graceful turn, but she also needs strength in her leg and stomach muscles.

4. FOR INTERMEDIATE SKIERS

The skier in the intermediate basic class usually covers stem turn, side-slipping, and the uphill christie. But, today, because of the increased speed of various teaching processes, we cover everything in this up to and including parallel christie and short swings.

Remember that confidence and progress in skiing go hand in hand. As the skier progresses, the V snowplow or stem position takes on less importance until it is eventually eliminated in parallel skiing. For the beginner who is aggressive, determined, or physically well coordinated, the period of snowplow and steered turns may be very brief, perhaps only a couple of days. Actually, whether it's snowplow, stem, or schwups, the steered turns remain a cornerstone on which most beginning skiers build technique—even GLM skiers do it on shorter skis. The skier puts his weight on the turning ski and uses it to steer his way in a new direction. Why does this turn—the object of so much criticism, since it creates a stemming habit that must be discarded later—have such an obstinate hold on skiing?

The reasons are twofold. First, it is essentially a turn that enables the skier to put a tight control on his speed at all times. For the beginner, speed equals fear and insecurity. Thus, by controlling speed in the steered turn, the learner gets rid of psychological factors that impede learning. Second, the steered turn can be done without the difficult timing of unweighting and upper-lower body coordination required in more advanced turns. The skier simply applies his weight to the curved side of the ski and effects a change of direction.

Now let's take a look at the turns and techniques that will lead to the expert class.

Stem Turn

The stem turn is essentially a snowplow turn with only one ski in the snowplow position (snowplows are sometimes called double stems).

As in the illustration, start with a traverse. Then stem your uphill ski while bringing your upper body "square" (that is, at a right angle) to the direction of travel. Gradually shift your weight to the stemmed ski. When the turn is completed, bring your inside ski next to the new downhill ski.

Forward Sideslip

Sideslipping is the basis of a great deal of advanced skiing. It's also an important safety maneuver. Faced with a slope that is too steep, the skier can sideslip down it without the risk of putting his skis into the fall line.

Starting from a traverse, sink down in your ankles and hips, and then come up to unweight your skis. At the same time, release (flatten) the ski edges. The result will be a slipping movement forward and downhill. With another sinking motion, reset your ski edges and return to a traverse.

Uphill Christie

The uphill christie isn't a complete turn. Rather, it is the closing portion of a number of turns. It also provides valuable practice in pushing the heels and, perfected, is a valuable means of stopping at high speeds, since the skis are turned *up* into the fall line.

As shown in the illustration above, start moving in a steep traverse, or straight down the fall line, and prepare by sinking down. You may plant your pole at this time. With an up motion, unweight your skis and displace them to one side to start the turn. Increase edging to control and encourage the turn. Reset the edges at the end of the down motion to complete the turn.

75

Stem Christie

The stem christie combines the elements of the stem turn and the uphill christie. Starting from the traverse, the turn starts exactly like a stem turn. But instead of holding the stem or V shape until the skis have completed the turn, the inside ski is brought parallel alongside the outside ski as soon as the skis start to turn. The rest of the turn is finished like an uphill christie. That is, from the traverse position, prepare to turn by stemming your uphill ski, turning your body to a position square to the direction of travel and sinking down. At this time you may also plant your inside pole. The actual turn is initiated with an up motion to unweight the skis and a transferal of your weight onto the outside ski. Immediately bring your inside ski alongside this turning (outside) ski. Control and encourage the turn by increasing the amount of edging as you gradually sink down. Set your edges at the end of the turn to complete the maneuver and to start a new traverse.

Parallel Christie

As you move across the hill in a traverse, prepare for the turn by sinking down while you square your upper body. The downhill pole may now be planted, if you use it. Immediately follow this with an up-forward motion, a change of your ski edges, and a transfer of your weight to the outside ski. During this unweighting phase, the turn is begun by displacing your skis to the outside. Gradually sink down throughout the turn, and complete it by resetting your edges into a new traverse.

Short Swing

Starting almost directly down the fall line, do short, rhythmic parallel christies, linking each turn without a traverse in between. These turns are done like the parallel christies, and checks may be added on steeper slopes.

Correct Upper Body Position

by JUNIOR BOUNOUS
Certified, Rocky Mountain Ski Instructors' Association

Many skiers change the position of their upper bodies too late in the turn. (You can often spot this kind of skier by his posed or stilted look.) Others use the same body position for turns in both directions. In either case, the weight transfer, if it comes at all, will be late, and the skier may fall to the inside or his tips may cross. Here, in a stem turn shown at the top of the following page, I lean to the inside of the turn. While I am able to make the turn, my left leg must be extended in order to put weight on it (second picture). Later I have trouble keeping my balance. Finally, in picture 4, I am leaning to the inside and my weight is on the uphill ski. From this position it is practically impossible to start the next turn.

In faster turns the leaning out or angulation of the upper body may be slight, but it must be there to give the skier balance. This is the key movement that lets the outside ski dominate and control the turn. It's the difference between riding the ski, which you can do when you angulate over it, and pushing against the ski, which you do when you lean to the inside. In the sequence at the bottom of the opposite page, I have started to tip my upper body out over the turning ski even before my skis reach the fall line. It's easy then to transfer my weight to the outside ski (picture 2) and stay in a comfortable position. In the last picture, I am balanced over my outside ski, ready to stem out for the next turn.

Tuck the Downhill Knee

by R. A. SOLBERG

In learning to snowplow and make stem turns, skiers are instructed to separate the feet and knees. As you progress, however, this open position of the legs actually becomes a hindrance in learning to traverse, sideslip, and make uphill turns. Here's a handy tip for getting rid of the open-legged stance.

Traverse across the hill with your uphill ski slightly ahead of the other ski. Next, tuck the downhill knee behind the uphill one. Now start to feel your legs, feet, and skis operating together as a unit. To emphasize the correct weighting over your downhill ski, lift the tail of the uphill ski a few inches off the snow as you cross the hill.

It should be emphasized that this isn't the correct position for skiing, but merely a drill or exercise.

Knee Flex—The Key to Easier Stem Turns

by JOAN TOWNE

After stemming the uphill ski and transferring weight to it, do you sometimes get a feeling that your ski still won't turn? This is often the result of stemming the uphill ski forward, and straightening and stiffening the uphill leg.

What you need is leverage to steer the outside ski around in a turn. You'll get it by carefully stemming the ski so that your knee is over its center and directly over or ahead of your boot. Now you can develop leverage to steer the outside ski in a turn simply by pressing forward on the front of your boot.

A Planted Pole Stays Down

by DIXI NOHL
Certified, Austrian Association of Professional Ski Instructors and U.S.
Eastern Amateur Ski Association

Some skiers aren't content to leave well enough alone. Having planted the downhill pole in readiness for the turn, they immediately think that they have to lift it out of the snow in order to turn. Result: their weight is set back, and the turn gets set back.

The correct method of pole retraction is simply to leave the basket resting in the snow. As you move forward and around, the pole will exit naturally from the snow. In this way, your arm will stay in a natural position, and your weight will be correctly distributed. Remember: to retract the pole, don't yank it out. Rather, leave it in the snow, feel the hand pushed forward, and let the basket come out of the snow naturally.

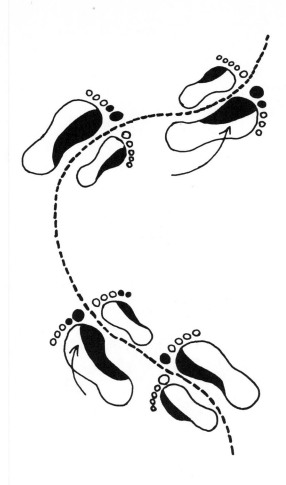

The Feel of Feet

by PETER PALMER
Certified, U.S. Eastern Amateur Ski Association

When you ski, think about your feet. Contemplating a turn, search for a feeling of pressure building up along the inside of the uphill ski boot. When you can feel pressure, the inside of your foot against the boot, step down and forward on that foot to turn the ski. It's just that simple!

As the outside ski carves out of the fall line, try to develop pressure along the inside ankle of the other boot to start a new turn. Feel the pressure, then turn.

Turn on Your Feet

by JOHN MCHALE

You ski with your feet, the final links between body and skis. To improve your technique, develop sensitivity in your feet; begin to feel how actions made by the upper body and lower body affect your feet. For instance, you can feel forward lean—the front of your ankles and shins press hard against the front of your boots; the balls of your feet are weighted. If you can feel these parts of your feet as you finish a turn, your skis are carving well. If you can't feel the front of your boots or the balls of your feet, you're just not pressing forward with your knees and your skis are slipping, not carving.

Beam Your Knee and See

by KERMIT LAMPLES
Certified, Canadian Ski Instructors' Alliance

While this idea will be useful to a skier of any turning ability, it is best illustrated in the stem turn. First think of the headlights on a car as they lead you around each turn of the road. Now, as you ski, imagine you have a headlight on your outside knee. Deliberately try to point the headlight in the direction of your turn. This conscious knee-pointing serves two important functions: (1) it emphasizes the weight over your outside knee and helps you keep it there; (2) it gives you a powerful sense of directional drive in your turn. Be sure to keep pointing the knee throughout the turn. You'll find that this awareness of the physical pressure created by your knee will help you steer stem turns.

Shift Your Weight Up and Forward

by PAUL R. BROWN
Certified, U.S. Eastern Amateur Ski Association

For a smoother stem christie, you should have a feeling that the upmotion, which unweights the skis, is also a forward motion. In this way your body weight will be able to keep up with the faster forward progress of your skis. By staying over your skis throughout the turn, you'll soon get a smoother, flowing movement and a more graceful stem christie.

Mini-Skids

by G. S. NELSON
Certified, Central Division, U.S. Ski Association

Because the speed of the traverse preceding an uphill christie often makes skiers uncomfortable, I teach my students "mini-skids," short sideslips that permit the skier to get the feel of an uphill christie without any fear of speed.

With both poles planted in the snow and the downhill pole several feet below your lower ski, step into a traverse about 30 to 40 degrees in declivity. Ask a friend to stand facing you with one of his pole baskets placed six inches behind your downhill ski tip. Then lean forward and flatten your skis, so that both ski tails begin to slide downhill. Your friend's pole will hold your ski tips in place. When your skis are perpendicular to the fall line, stop the slide by resetting the edges of your skis. Repeat this exercise several times until you can do it without using your poles for balance.

Pull the Knees Up to Unweight

by DIXI NOHL

Certified, Austrian Association of Professional Ski Instructors and U.S. Eastern Amateur Ski Association

Until you've reached the advanced stages of parallel skiing, the normal way to start your skis into a turn is to unweight them with an up motion. The easiest way is with a simple hop; you sink down, come up to unweight, then sink down again. Many beginning parallel skiers, however, do this incorrectly. They straighten their whole bodies in a vigorous attempt to hop. The result is an unstable, straight-legged position at the top of the up motion. This is wrong. Rather, when you are unweighting you should think of pulling just your knees up toward the upper body. This will leave your knees slightly flexed at the top of the unweighting, giving you more stability and a more fluid-looking turn.

Down into the Hill

by OTHMAR SCHNEIDER

To review for a moment, the uphill christie is made as follows: Slowly traverse across a slope, with your feet separated about six inches. Then, springing from your ankles and knees, hop up and forward. Land softly, bending your knees. You'll find that your skis skid sideways and then carve into the hill, producing a turn without a stem. Don't try to do this on a slope that is bowl-shaped, as this makes extra work.

94

To christie down into the hill, an uphill christie can be performed with a down-unweighting motion. Unlike up-unweighting, you start out standing very high and then drop down abruptly to produce a skid of your ski tails and a carve into the hill. Be sure to project this down movement forward; a sitting position will not produce a turn into the hill.

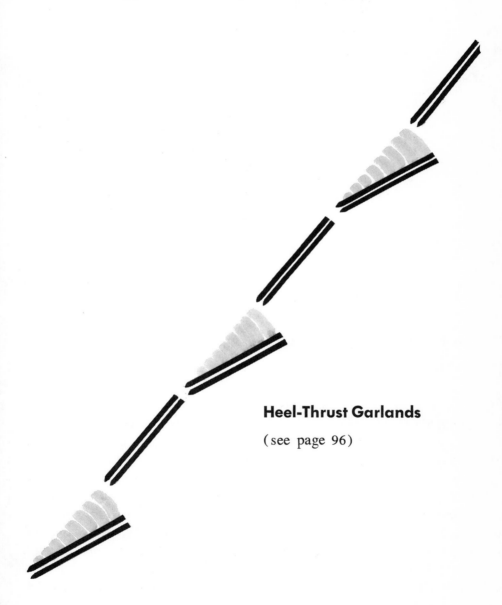

Heel-Thrust Garlands

(see page 96)

Heel-Thrust Garlands

by OTHMAR SCHNEIDER

Doing a faster christie-down-into-the-hill—with a down-unweighting motion and with some physical force put into the downhill push of your ski tails—produces a series of short turns into the hill. Traverse across a convex slope with your body upright, then sink down quickly, but be sure to keep your hip uphill. This sinking movement causes your ski tails to slide sideways, but you quickly edge them by pointing your knees into the hill. Spring up again to get your skis back on the traverse. Repeat these movements and try to do a series of garlands across the slope. Don't stop if your first few attempts are not satisfactory; eventually you will combine all the movements correctly. You are doing garlands correctly if your skis leave a track in the snow like that on page 95.

Knee Wobbles

by JOHN WINN

Certified, U.S. Eastern Amateur Ski Association

To become an expert skier, it's necessary to learn how to set and release your ski edges with ease. To get my edges biting, I often practice the following exercise.

On a moderately steep, packed slope, I start "knee wobbles" in a traverse. You can try it, too. Roll your knees toward the bottom of the hill as you rise up slightly and flatten your edges to slide sideways. When you feel your skis sideslipping, reset your edges with a slight sinking motion, rolling your knees back into the hill. Repeat these two maneuvers and then again—slide, set, slide, set. . . . When you learn to do knee wobbles with finesse, you'll be able to see a pattern to the tracks left behind you in the snow, as illustrated here. With a little practice you'll be able to execute rapid edge sets in a traverse just by wobbling your knees without unweighting your skis.

Use a Skater's Stop

by ALLEN PEERY

Associate Certification, Pacific Northwest Ski Instructors' Association

Control of speed in short swing and wedeln comes in part from a proper setting of the skis' edges. If you're having trouble setting your edges, try making some simple, abrupt stop turns. With skis pointing downhill and feet in a comfortable, wide stance, pick up speed and hop both skis abruptly across the fall line to skid to a sudden stop. Head and shoulders should be facing toward the bottom of the hill, while your hips and knees will press uphill, causing the skis to edge sharply. This is a position iden-

tical to the one adopted by a skater when he comes to an abrupt stop. It is also pretty much the same body position you should have at the edge-set phase of a short swing turn on steep terrain.

By remembering to keep your upper body generally facing down the hill, you will skid into each edge set and link your short turns down the fall line—under control.

Search for Ankle Pressure

by PETER PALMER
Certified, U.S. Eastern Amateur Ski Association

To develop a better feel for inside ankle pressure practice a series of step-over turns. On shallow terrain, start from a narrow V and step quickly from one ski's inside edge to the inside edge of the opposite ski. With each step, try to build up pressure between the inside of your ankle and your boot. As illustrated here, on steeper terrain, each stepover feels more like a hop, and skis become parallel between steps. Step over to one ski and create inside ankle pressure; then, quickly step down and forward on the same foot to start the ski turning. As soon as you can feel a turn begin, rise up and step over again to the opposite ski edge, and so on.

The Paddle Brake Turn

by RUEDI WYRSCH

Certified, Swiss National Ski School and U.S. Eastern Amateur Ski Association

In the modern carved turn on ice or hardpack, the skier has to execute a powerful knee push into the hill to keep the edges carving. The upper body meanwhile remains fairly square over the skis. This is a turn for advanced skiers, but a reasonably good skier can get a feel for it with what I call "the canoe paddle brake turn." It is a quick way to learn the advanced carved turn.

Imagine you are sitting in a canoe coasting along a lake. If you put your right paddle in the water, lean to the left at the hip, and brake your forward motion with the paddle, the canoe will turn sharply to the right. The same principle will apply to skis. Point your skis down the fall line and start moving. Plant both poles together about a foot away from the right ski and a foot ahead of the boot. The result will be to brake your forward slide, and both skis will turn instantly to the right. The very sudden turn will upset your balance slightly. To correct this, you will instinctively move your outside hip back, your knees will twist into the hill. Try a series of these canoe paddle turns. They will give you the feel of pushing your knees into the hill.

A

B

Slide Out of a Stem

by TED CLARK
Examiner, Canadian Ski Instructors' Alliance

A stem in skiing is as difficult to eliminate as a slice in golf. Breaking either habit requires a conscious effort and lots of practice.

To kick the stemming habit (*A*), try to change and improve your body position at the beginning of each turn. Slide the downhill ski forward so that it is even with the uphill ski (*B*). Pushing the downhill ski forward will place your feet closer together and your body in a far better position to unweight both skis in a good parallel turn. By reprogramming your lower leg to do something different, you'll eventually get rid of your stem. Then you'll find it easier to learn more advanced ski maneuvers with a good, natural body position and feet together.

Steepen Your Traverse

by NORM SAVAGE
Certified, Canadian Ski Instructors' Alliance

Difficult problems often have easy solutions. This is a statement applicable to many stem christie, hop christie, and parallel skiers who have difficulty initiating turns. Usually it is a question of getting the skis started downhill in the direction of the turn.

Inability to start a turn may be caused by the fact that your traverse is too shallow before the turn. The traverse may be so shallow that when you transfer your weight out onto the uphill ski it still will not start down the hill. Result? At slow speeds you'll be unable to get your skis to turn downhill. To get the tails of your skis to shift around, you'll have to push them uphill, almost impossible when you're skiing slowly.

Therefore, point your skis more downhill as you prepare for the turn. Thus, when you step your weight onto the turning ski, it will already be in the fall line. A gravity heel thrust plus the momentum of additional speed will easily complete the turn.

Off the Fall Line for Intermediates

by Dixi Nohl
Certified, Austrian Association of Professional Ski Instructors and U.S. Eastern Amateur Ski Association

In Chapter 2, I described several maneuvers for beginners. Here are two for intermediates:

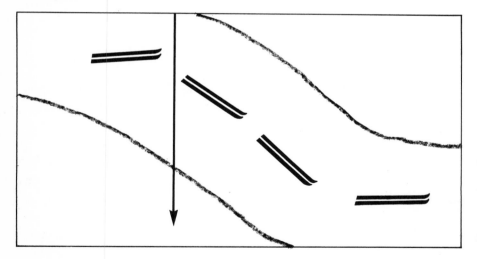

Rolling Sideslip

Begin by doing the open-stance sideslip, as described on page 62, but when you have gained speed, edge your skis and bend forward in your knees so that you start to move uphill slightly. When you slow down,

106

raise your body and lean back to put some weight on the tails of your skis. This will cause the tips to drift downhill. Let them run until you feel you are moving fast enough, then push your knees forward quickly, and bend your ankles again as you thrust your ski tails downhill. You will start moving uphill into the slope again. Repeat this in a rhythmic, rolling motion.

Flying Stem

Add some variety to the rolling sideslip by occasionally stemming out the uphill ski. From the sideslip position described above, simply raise your body, and at the same time push out the uphill ski into a slight snowplow and head down the fall line. When you begin to gather speed, slide the skis together, bend your knees, and thrust the tails downhill—let the skis carry you uphill again. Repeat this flying stem at different speeds, depending on the width of the slope and your own inclinations.

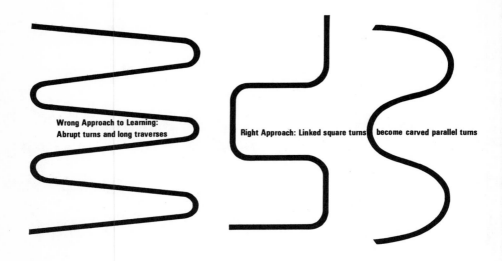

Wrong Approach to Learning: Abrupt turns and long traverses

Right Approach: Linked square turns become carved parallel turns

Ease Fall-Line Fear

by WILLIAM BRIGGS

Certified, U.S. Eastern Amateur Ski Association, Far West Ski Instructors' Association, Intermountain Ski Instructors' Association

Fear of skiing straight down the fall line from a parallel turn causes many beginning parallel skiers to make abrupt sideslipped turns between lengthy traverses.

To ease fear of the fall line, practice "square turns." Stand across a hill and plant both poles to hop your skis into the fall line so that the tips point straight downhill. Ski down the fall line at least one ski length before carving a gradual turn out of the fall line. When you reach a complete stop, hop your ski tips in the fall line again to make another square turn. Start first on gentle terrain, advancing to intermediate and even expert trails. Then, link square turns to each other by hopping from a slow traverse into the fall line for each turn. Gradually round off the corners of your square turns as you lose fear of skiing in the fall line and learn to carve rounded parallel turns.

Stop the Stem Before It Starts

by ROB VERRILL
Certified, U.S. Eastern Amateur Ski Association

Beginning parallel skiers often sit or squat over their skis at the start of each turn. When the skier's weight is too far back on the tail of his skis, the lower ski often slips downhill into a slight stem.

To curb a tendency to stem, exaggerate bending forward at the ankles during the down-motion and pole-plant phase of the turn. Feel your ankles pressing hard against the front of your ski boots. Keeping your weight forward as you plant your pole will help prevent a stem from occurring at the beginning of each turn. When you press against the front of your boots at the start of the turn, you'll find it much easier to keep your feet together.

Be Sure Your Skis Move Sideways

by M. J. FLUTEY
Certified, Canadian Ski Instructors' Alliance

Remember that the two essential ingredients for initiating any parallel turn are: (1) to unweight the skis; and (2) to be able to move them laterally across the snow to change direction.

Few skiers experience much difficulty in learning how to bounce on the skis to unweight them. But many skiers fail to get their bodies in a properly angulated position so that the skis can be pushed sideways to set the platform for launching the turn. Angulation also is needed to push the skis uphill and to the outside for the turn itself.

In *A* in the illustration, for instance, the skier is unweighting. But because he is in an erect, unangulated position, the effect is simply to push the skis down into the snow, since his legs and hips are directly above

them. No change in the direction takes place. But in figure *B,* the skier's body is angulated and his hips are no longer centered over the skis. Thus, as the skier bounces to unweight, his skis can move laterally to set a platform, then rebound sideways to turn in the new direction. This lateral "wagging" back and forth of the lower legs is only possible with proper angulation. Coordination with unweighting is what makes parallel turns of this kind possible.

A

"Peek Around the Barn"

by Tom Mulkern
Certified, U.S. Eastern Amateur Ski Association

Beginning parallel skiers often have a tendency to sideslip through the finish of their turns, leaning uphill. To correct this common fault and eliminate unwanted sideslip, try the following visual aid.

Make a single parallel turn around an imaginary blind corner, such as a barn. While turning, try to peek around this make-believe barn, bending your head and shoulders downhill out over your lower ski so that your line of vision is on or below the tips of your skis.

With your upper body already bent downhill to peer around the blind corner, you'll find it easy to begin pressing with your knees up and in toward the hill to set your skis on their edges, carving a smooth, controlled arc.

Tap, Tap, Tap, and Turn

by GORDON WEST
Certified, Pacific Northwest Ski Instructors' Association

In a traverse on gradual terrain, use the downhill pole and wrist action to make consecutive pole plants in the snow. Simply pick at the terrain below the ski shovels, emphasizing wrist action to manipulate the pole. Let the last pick in the traverse trigger a new parallel turn and immediately begin picking with the new downhill pole.

Besides eliminating unnecessary arm movements to streamline pole action, you'll improve your body position. When you reach downhill to produce each series of pole picks, you'll lessen any tendency to lean uphill in a traverse.

115

Hop Sideways, Not Up

by HAROLD HERBERT

Certified, Rocky Mountain Ski Instructors' Association

Like the backswing in golf or the swinging back of the leg before kicking a football, the check in skiing is used as a preparatory motion for the turn. The skier "sets" his edges on an imaginary platform on the snow and then bounces from the knees so that the skis unweight and can be easily swung in the new direction of the turn.

Many beginning parallel skiers make the mistake of assuming that the hop from the check is straight up in the air. It is not. Hopping vertically may get the weight off the skis, but it will not move them sideways in the direction you want to turn. After making the check, hop the skis sideways. Then you'll come down on your skis and carve your turn in the new direction.

"Gorilla Hop" to Parallel

by M<small>ARY</small> A<small>NNE</small> D<small>AY</small>
Certified, Pacific Northwest Ski Instructors' Association

Good muscle coordination—perhaps the result of excelling in another sport—often enables beginning skiers to make parallel turns early. If you are unusually well coordinated and in good physical condition, try making parallel turns by hopping your skis across the fall line to turn. Starting from a wide-track traverse, plant your lower pole in the snow. Quickly, hop several inches off the snow and twist your skis in the direction of the fall line. When you land, hop again, turning your skis in the same direction. Two or three hops should bring you around the turn. When you cross the fall line be sure to land with most of your weight on the new downhill ski.

Your first attempts may be quite awkward, but if you are able to turn in this manner, continue practicing "gorilla hops" until you can change direction with a single hop. Eventually, you will be able to eliminate the hop entirely, making smooth parallel turns with only a small up motion to unweight your skis.

Stop Depending on Your Poles

by HUBERT VOGEL

A beginning parallel skier frequently leans on his pole after planting it, often leaving it in the snow throughout the entire turn. The result is that by the end of the turn the planted pole has pulled the skier's uphill shoulder back, so that he is facing uphill. Thus he is out of position for the next turn.

If you've become overly dependent on your poles, try grabbing them about three-quarters of the way up the shaft, as illustrated here. From a traverse, reach out to plant your pole downhill just as you start the turn. But don't plant the pole! Simply rise up to unweight your skis, and sink down to finish the turn. Then reach out again to plant the downhill pole, but again don't plant it! To start each turn with a good platform, be sure to place more weight on the downhill ski each time you sink down and reach out. Practice this exercise until you kick the habit of leaning on your pole.

A Perfect Ending to a Parallel Turn

by RUEDI WYRSCH

Certified, Swiss National Ski School and U.S. Eastern Amateur Ski Association

Keeping the skis together at the end of a parallel turn is often difficult, because most skiers have a tendency to rotate their hips in the direction of the turn. When this happens, a skier's weight usually ends up on his uphill ski and his lower ski tail slips out into a stemmed position.

Use your own imagination to help stop hip rotation. At the end of your turns, try sitting on an imaginary stool set into the snow uphill from your ski boots. If you concentrate on making contact with the stool, you'll learn to turn your uphill hip forward and hold the lower hip back. You'll also flex your knees to sit—a perfect ending to a parallel turn.

Instant Wedeln

by GEORGES JOUBERT

With the new designs in skis and boots, and from what we've learned from today's top racers, it's become increasingly easy to teach people to make wedeln turns in the early stages of skiing. As a matter of fact, I've recently been successful in getting half of my college-age beginners to do the simple wedeln turn shown here after only two hours of instruction.

Here's how. Start by forgetting that you need to turn with your feet together as the experts do. With your feet comfortably apart, turn by pushing off from one foot onto the other. In the first figure, the skier has most of his weight on the left ski. He pushes off on this leg to unweight his body from the snow. During the brief instant of unweighting he steers both skis around in the direction of the new turn. As the body's weight is reapplied to the snow, the skier absorbs it with his right ski, which is edged. The shape of the ski helps to steer the turn farther around. To start a new turn, the skier simply repeats these actions, using his poles to help the pushing off from one ski to the other. We call this "steering" with the outside leg. Execute a series of the turns in a slow rhythm, with each turn taking two to three seconds. It also helps if you turn without pushing your weight over the skis. Sitting a little will help you utilize the rear of your skis, which will make these turns easier.

"Shadow Ski" Your Way to Better Form

by JERRY DUNN
Certified, Central Division, U.S. Ski Association

Nature provides you with a way of looking at yourself as you ski down the hill. On a bright day, when the sun is behind you and not too high in the sky, you'll be clearly able to see a shadow of your body moving on the snow. You can use this to your advantage, just as a good fighter shadowboxes to sharpen his punching. For instance, how often have you thought you were skiing perfectly parallel, only to hear the instructor yell: "You're still stemming your ski." "Shadow skiing" can clearly illustrate this and other faults you may have. And for a real comparison, try shadow skiing down the hill with an instructor or a very good skier at your side. You'll be able to compare your shadow with his, and by imitative action and correction rapidly improve your ski form.

5.   FOR EXPERT SKIERS

When you enter the expert class, you'll start thinking more about techniques. Each winter seems to bring us a new ski technique, a final solution of how to turn a pair of skis. Each new technique is hailed as a revolution; old techniques are cast in the dust. In the 1950s, skiers were told to discard rotation in favor of reverse shoulder action. In the 1960s, we were told to discard reverse shoulder for anticipation, in which the upper torso is turned in the direction of the turn, almost like old-fashioned rotation! For years we were told to get our weight forward. Now, for a split instant, we are told to sit back for avalement.

Where does the truth lie? Does a skier need to keep changing his technique? Are the old turns obsolete? The answers are both yes and no. Yes, a good skier should learn the new techniques like avalement because, quite obviously, they will make him a better skier and enable him to take advantage of the vast improvements in the new boots and skis. No, the old turns are not obsolete: Some are essential to learning how to ski; others are especially useful for certain kinds of snow and terrain conditions.

Watch a racer go down a slalom course and you'll see him employ a whole repertoire of turns: step turns, reverse shoulder, anticipation, jet turns with avalement. He's not making a conscious effort to vary his turns—step here, jet there. Rather, he's gone to school and is now the pure athlete. He's making optimum use of all the techniques that have been developed to change direction. And so should you.

Here's a catalogue of the turns that an expert skier should have in his repertoire.

The Simple Step

The most direct way to change direction on skis is simply to step the skis, a little at a time. In the illustration here, the skier is moving at a slow speed down the hill. To turn across the hill, he steps his inside ski, then brings the other one alongside. The step is repeated to increase the change of direction.

This kind of turn is so common in usage that it often seems ignored. It can be used to avoid obstacles and other skiers on the hill and to change direction quickly in slalom. It is one of the most common turns in cross-country skiing, and it helps many skiers turn in deep, cementlike snow. Stepping is also the normal way to change your face of direction in a stationary position. For a classic use, watch a skier using it to move ahead stealthily in the lift line.

Above all, the simple step is important for developing balance and ambidextrousness in both feet.

Pure Rotation

This is the turn that is the mother of them all. Even though Anton Seelos began doing it back in the 1930s, it has lost none of its beauty in the forty years it's been around.

In the sequence illustrated here, demonstrator Fowler executes the rotation with a nonclassic down motion to initiate the turn. The essence of the turn is to use a rotational movement of the upper torso to power the change of direction. This power of rotation is transmitted to the legs by a blocking action of the hips. Actually, it's a contraction of the abdominal muscles that acts as a clutch, transferring the rotation of the upper body to the legs. Here, on the opposite page, the demonstrator feels the rotation of the upper body, led by the hand and shoulder, lock to his stomach muscles and act on his legs and feet all the way through the turn. The trick is to avoid overrotation without blockage, thereby using up the rotary power when the turn is only half complete.

Rotation is still a practical turn for all kinds of deep snow. But best of all, when executed by a good skier it is an elegant, fluid turn that imparts a wonderful feeling to the whole body. What a relief from those choppy little turns down the fall line!

The Pure Reverse or Counterrotation

This is a wonderful theoretical turn—with some interesting practical applications—built on the third law of the eighteenth-century physicist, Sir Isaac Newton. The law states that for every action there is an equal or opposite reaction. Applied to the reverse-rotation ski turn, it works in this way.

The skier (see sequence) goes up to unweight his skis from the snow. He rotates his legs and skis downhill to make his change of direction. This rotary action is made possible by an opposing reaction of the shoulders, which move the other way.

This kind of turn became popular in the 1950s, a time when ski instruction experts used the analogy of a man standing on a piano stool: if he rotates his feet in one direction, his shoulders rotate the other way, and vice versa. The reverse shoulder or counterrotation theory became the basis for explaining the new Austrian wedeln or tail-wagging—a series of short turns down the fall line in which the shoulders are reversed from the direction of the turn.

As demonstrated in a pure reverse turn on the next page by Corky Fowler, the shoulders stay reversed throughout the turn. It puts him in an extreme "comma" position, with a sharp, biting carve of the skis—somewhat unstable, but interesting to look at and to do.

Because counterrotation turns only work easily where the skis meet little or no resistance to turning from the snow, they are desirable in all kinds of turns that involve extreme up-weighting or skis in the air. This makes it a good turn for a bouncy, up-and-down flight through the bumps. It's also used for quick-punch turns in slalom or tight maneuvers in bumps. If you want to see extreme reverse, watch a racer making a recovery turn.

The Split-Rotation Turn: Two Ways

"Why can't I just learn one way to turn?" It's a question many skiers ask after they've gotten beyond the beginning stage. And, in a simplistic way, too, many ski lesson promoters have tried to sell them one solution. But there is no simple panacea. The human body is a complex, dynamic machine that finds itself in as many different positions as a turn needs to be made on the hill. The answer is not to make one kind of turn every time, but to answer the more urgent needs. Be prepared and avoid falling. The good skier is one who responds to snow, terrain, and the situation at hand, not someone who imposes his technique on the hill.

The continued popularity of split rotation which came into use a decade ago, arises out of the adaptability it gives the skier. Like most techniques it got its start in racing. Now it can be used by anybody.

In the sequence on the opposite page, you see Corky Fowler performing the two basic variations of split-rotation. At the top of the page, he starts turning by rotation, then, as the turn progresses, he reverses his shoulders to the direction of the turn. (By comparing the rotate-to-reverse sequence here with the anticipation with edge set on page 136, you can observe the slight difference at the beginning of the turn.)

In the second sequence at the bottom of the page, Fowler initiates the turn with counterrotation, then completes it with a nice round rotary movement, body square to the skis.

The varied situations in which split rotation can be used are too numerous to catalogue. Here are a couple of examples. You are rounding out a nice turn across the hill, body square over your skis. All of a sudden you need to make a quick turn to avoid a skier. Quickly, up motion, twist the skis under you, and reverse your shoulders. Then you round out the turn leisurely, complete it with rotation. Another situation. You're in the middle of a long, rotated turn and suddenly you spot a rock ahead. Quickly, angulate your body, lead with the downhill shoulder, and complete a sharp turn with counterrotation or reverse.

Truly an adaptable turn!

A

B

The Mambo

Pure playful rhythm, mambo is a series of turns linked together so smoothly it looks like milk pouring from a bottle in slow motion. The challenge of mambo is how well you can defy gravity and get away with it. Here's how demonstrator Fowler describes it.

"As demonstrated here, I start on a relatively gentle slope and gain enough speed to overcome the resistance of the snow. From the fall line, the first turn starts with a down and forward motion while the upper body is rotating and leaning slightly in the direction of the first turn. Arms are held shoulder high and wide for balance.

"The skis start turning slowly at first, then quickly cross the hill. I overrotate so far that I must start rotating in the other direction before I fall over. For a split second, while the skis are turning one way and the body is initiating a turn the other way, you'll glimpse the classic reverse shoulder position. But it's only a glimpse. Unless I keep moving into the new rotated direction, I'll fall over.

"It's simply a continuous twisting and untwisting to a rhythm. Make the rhythm long and you can climb the side of a gully, hang suspended for a moment in reverse position and then fall, rotating gracefully into the finish of the turn back into the gully and up the other side. Make the rhythm short and you can wind through bumps like a snake."

The Ruade

Here's a museum piece of a ski turn that still has its uses. The ruade (literally, "horse kick") was popularized in the late 1940s by the great French technician, Emile Allais. Using both poles, the skier stays forward and kicks the tails of the skis in the air from side to side, like a horse kicking his heels. It's a good turn to know the next time you find yourself on a steep slope in mashed potatoes or ice-crusted snow, or in a narrow, uninviting gully that must be skied.

The Foot Swivel Off a Bump

Here is one of the easiest turns in all of skiing, yet few people stop to practice it. It's used frequently, and almost unawares, by good skiers in mogul fields. But its principal advantage is that it is an ideal way to show beginners and many advanced-intermediate skiers how to learn anticipation, thereby putting them on the route to modern ski technique.

An ideal learning turn is one—like the steered or short ski turn— which avoids the need for the skier to overcome a multiplicity of psychological factors and coordinated body movements and allows him to concentrate on just one or two things in the split second a turn occurs. The advantage of a foot swivel off the top of a bump is that it eliminates the immediate need to coordinate unweighting with turning. It puts the tips and tails of the skis in the air and concentrates all of the skier's weight on one pivot point under his feet.

To illustrate this, place a pencil lengthwise on your desk, apply some pressure on it, and note the resistance it creates when you try to turn it. Now take the same pencil and hold it firmly, point down, on the desk: you can turn it with no effort. This is the equivalent in a ski turn of being atop a bump and so getting rid of the snow's resistance to turning.

In the sequence illustrated here note the skier's position before he reaches the top of the bump. His head and shoulders are facing downhill anticipating the direction of the turn. There's a lot of coiled energy stored in that body: why doesn't it cause the skis to turn? Because the tips and tails of the skis are on the snow and resist the turning action. But now, in the next figure, demonstrator Fowler is on top of the bump, the tips and tails (although you can't see the latter) are off the snow, and the coiled energy in his legs is permitted to twist the skis in the new direction.

Anticipation with Edge Set: The Jet Turn

Here, with a French accent, is the classic turn of our time. It bridges the 1960s and 1970s with the kind of domination that the Austrian wedeln exerted on the 1950s. It is a turn, with changing emphasis, that will get you down any hill and through most kinds of snow: perfect for controlling your speed down the steepest slopes, good for ice, snaky, easy for moguls, and the acknowledged route to more advanced turning with avalement.

Anticipation with edge set initially caused some confusion, because many skiers thought it was a return to rotation. But closer analysis reveals it to be another way to initiate a change of direction. If you studied the earlier illustration in this section showing foot swivel on a bump, you understand how anticipation works. In this case, the top of the bump is replaced by a flexing and unflexing of the legs. This action unweights the skis and reduces their resistance to turning from the snow.

As an analogy, hold a piece of spring wire at the two ends. Twist one end while holding the other steady. You are now illustrating what happens just before the ski turn takes place: The upper body is twisted in the direction of the turn, but the feet—the other end of the wire—resist turning because the skis are solidly planted in the snow by the edge set. To continue the analogy, release your fingers from the fixed end of the spring wire. It untwists rapidly in the direction in which you had twisted the other end.

You have now illustrated what happens when unweighting releases pressure of the skis on the snow. Their resistance to turning has been alleviated and the feet are permitted to twist in the direction of the turn.

In making this turn, watch for two things. First, the way the pole is planted is important. The pole should not be planted by reaching forward, but rather by extending the pole more laterally and down the hill with your hand. Second, you should be able to feel a tendency of the feet to shoot or "jet" forward slightly as the pressure of the skis is released from the snow. As a result, turns of this kind have been christened *jet turns*. It is an action that becomes increasingly important as the skier moves toward the more advanced technique of modern skiing.

The Turn with "Avalement"

There's a school of thinking in the sport that says that all skiing is simply a series of controlled changes of direction down the hill. The operative word here is "controlled." And the key to control is to keep the skis in contact with the snow. That's what avalement—a French word that means "swallowing"—is all about. The skier swallows up irregularities in the terrain, like bumps, by a folding and unfolding action of his legs, which act as shock absorbers. In this way, his skis stay in contact with the snow, turns are carved throughout, and the upper body travels in the shortest and most efficient line down the hill.

You see this in the sequence of demonstrator Fowler as he executes a turn with anticipation, incorporating avalement over the top of a bump. As he reaches the bump his legs fold up so that he appears to sit back for an instant. This is the movement of avalement. As a result of the leg retraction, which swallows up the up-unweighting effect of the bump, the skis are not thrown in the air, but remain in contact with the down side of the bump to make the turn. He also has accentuated the jetting action of the skis described earlier. The feet are pushed forward in the direction of the turn.

Turns with avalement are especially good for bumps, for continuous turning control on ice, and for deep snow.

Unweighting for Advanced Skiers

by OTHMAR SCHNEIDER

While ski techniques may come and go, one fundamental remains: you must get your weight off a ski to make it turn. There are different ways of doing this, and there are nuances and variations within those ways, but the one constant is to unweight in order to eliminate the friction that prevents the skis from turning on the snow.

There are two deliberate ways to unweight yourself. One is by up-unweighting, a down-up-down motion by which you push your weight off the snow. The second is down-unweighting, a kind of unweighting that is accomplished by dropping your body quickly. (You can see the effect of this kind of unweighting on a bathroom scale: as you quickly flex your knees, the needle on the scale will dip briefly.) Up-unweighting is easier to learn, is more graceful in certain kinds of turn, and is good for heavy snow. Down-unweighting is harder to learn because of the split-second timing needed to coordinate the brief period of unweighting with the turning of the skis. But it is quick, it is good on ice because the skis stay more in contact with the ground, and it'll keep you from being bucked into the air by bumps.

A really good skier uses both types of unweighting, and mixes them with ease for better control, variety, and fun. Here are three ways for the advanced skier to practice unweighting and have his fun.

Run and Hop and Skid

In the "gorilla-hop" maneuver described on page 117, the skier bends down and hops up, lifting the tails of his skis. Now, using a gentle slope and skiing straight toward the bottom of the hill, make the same hop, but add a sideways movement of your ski tails with each hop. It's not as easy as it looks, but with vigorous movements you should be able to produce a pattern in the snow like the one above. From this exercise (actually, on the intermediate ability level), you can progress to doing the fall line turns described below.

Parallel with Hop

Next you can apply the run-and-hop-and-skid exercise to wide-arc-ing parallel turns. Traverse across a gentle slope and hop up to unweight your skis. As the tails of the skis are lifted, push them uphill. Land softly and point your knees downhill in the direction of the turn. Throughout this turn keep your knees bent, with feet parallel and comfortably separated. Once you have tried this turn in both directions, link a series of them.

Fall Line Turns

To make many rapid turns directly down the fall line of a steeper slope, you need to push the tails of your skis to one side across the fall line, check by turning your edges into the hill, and then abruptly unweight with an up movement. You can easily turn your skis during this rebound. At first, do this unweighting with a hop, but gradually let it smooth out, so that your skis are almost touching the snow throughout the turn.

Keep your body facing downhill during the entire turn and keep it moving up and forward in the direction of the fall line. As you set your edges, plant your pole well down the fall line. Note that you can borrow the checking movements of your ski edges from the heel-thrust garland maneuver described for intermediate skiers on page 96.

143

A

Start Off on the Right Foot

by STAN CZARNIAK
Certified, U.S. Eastern Amateur Ski Association

A parallel skier who consistently starts off his turns with good edge sets and pole plants will usually make better ski runs than a skier who is careless in his approaches to parallel turns. Skier A's approach is to lean uphill, transferring his weight to the uphill ski as he plants his pole in the snow. When he leans uphill, his lower ski tail unfortunately slips out into a stemmed position. Right from the start he has reduced his chances of finishing the turn with his skis parallel.

Skier B increases his upper-body lean toward the bottom of the hill and sets his ski edges into the snow as he plants his pole.

To eliminate any tendency you might have to let your lower ski slide downhill, practice increasing your weight over the downhill ski as you plant your pole. This exercise will help you start each turn properly and will increase your chances for completing all of your parallel turns in good style.

B

Be a "Falling Body"

by CORKY FOWLER

Intermediate parallel skiers often reach a plateau from which further progress seems slow and insignificant. To execute a breakthrough into advanced phases of the sport, you must learn to flow with the terrain and slope of the hill instead of fighting gravity by leaning uphill.

When you ski, you're a falling body and that's what skiing is all about. Next time you are up for some practice, look for a moderate slope with a few small bumps. Approach one on a traverse (*A*). Release your ski edges to initiate the turn and allow your upper body to fall downhill—forward and in the direction of the turn (*B*). Just fall (*C*), don't force or muscle the motion.

As your edges change on the snow, your body weight will remain over your skis in perfect balance. Feel yourself drawn into the turn as you fall downhill. The turn will require much less energy because your body weight doesn't resist the change in direction. Try it!

Turn Your Head Before You Turn

by DON LEMOS
Certified, Rocky Mountain Ski Instructors' Association

Expert skiers pay careful attention to the terrain they ski on to achieve their best runs. Many intermediates, however, have a tendency to look away from the hill, or down at the tips of their skis, instead of watching the skiable terrain. Here's a surprisingly easy tip to improve your skiing.

As you prepare for each turn by bringing your pole forward to plant, turn your head in the direction of the anticipated turn. Check out the terrain below where your turn will be executed. Twisting your neck during the preparatory phase of the turn also encourages a proper upper body position. Try turning your head before each turn and watch your skiing improve.

148

To Close Your Skis, Separate Your Knees

by KAREN KUNKEL
Certified, Central Division, U.S. Ski Association

Many women skiers have difficulty learning to ski pure parallel. There is often a trace of stem at the start of each turn that stubbornly persists year after year, despite most efforts to remove it.

Because many women are slightly knock-kneed, concentration on skiing with knees together often enlarges the problem. A knock-kneed skier setting her edges in a down motion actually forces her lower leg out into a stem.

If you have a tendency to ski with your knees together while your feet drift apart, practice skiing with a slight space between your knees. You'll discover that skiing with your knees just a few inches apart enables you to set your edges to start a turn without forcing your lower leg into a stemmed position.

Swing Like a Pendulum

by BUD UMBARGER
Certified, Far West Ski Instructors' Association

Until a few years ago, ski techniques in vogue relied heavily on the force of the upper body to turn a pair of skis. However, because of recent improvements in ski equipment—higher, stiffer boots and softer skis—most experts today depend on the lower body—hips, knees, and ankles—for more precise turning power.

To develop strong turning action with your lower body, imagine you are a grandfather clock. Ski with your head up like a stationary clock face and let your feet swing from side to side like a rhythmic pendulum. Rely on your lower body for turning power by pushing your knees forcefully forward—out of the fall line and up the hill—to carve each new turn. Make short turns in the fall line. Keep your head up and your upper body facing downhill, and use your shoulders to maintain good balance and edge control, not to turn your skis.

A New Way to Measure Pole Length

by STEFAN NAGEL

Certified, U.S. Eastern Amateur Ski Association

Modern ski techniques place much importance on pole planting for both long parallel turns and short swing. However, many advanced skiers have limited success assimilating the latest refinements into their own skiing because their ski poles are too long. Long poles tend to set a skier's weight back on his heels and interfere with setting up a good rhythm for short swing.

The old rule of thumb—that poles should reach up to the armpit—is obsolete, in the opinion of many instructors who now advocate shorter poles, particularly for advanced skiers. To check for proper pole length, place the tip of your pole in the snow as if you were about to make a turn. If your poles are short enough, the wrist-to-elbow section of your arm will be parallel to the ground. Checking proper length in a ski shop or in your home, place the pole grips on the floor, grasping the shafts just below their baskets. Again, your lower arm should run parallel to the floor.

Double-Pole Power

by JANET NELSON
Certified, Canadian Ski Instructors' Alliance

Ever have a day when you can't seem to get going? Normally you're a pretty good skier, but some days you bounce off moguls, lose control on steep slopes, and fall on easy trails.

There could be a variety of reasons for your bad day. However, there's one trick that puts most skiers right back on their feet—double-poling. At the instant when you would normally plant your downhill pole to trigger the turn, plant both poles in the snow. This action gets you forward on your skis and forces you to bend your knees and ankles. More important, double-poling gets your mind on something besides the slope. Do the double-pole exercise forcefully and soon you'll be relaxed and skiing like your old self. Then you can resume normal pole action with single-pole plants.

153

Keep Your Hands Where You Can See Them

by D<small>AVE</small> W<small>ILEY</small>

Certified, Pacific Northwest Ski Instructors' Association

If you learn to ski so that both hands stay within your peripheral vision, you'll cure most tendencies to overreverse or overrotate your upper body.

If you are inclined to use an extreme reverse comma position (*A*), so that too much weight falls on the tails of your skis, simply bring your lower hand ahead, within your peripheral vision. This will correct your upper body position and help bring your weight forward, over your skis.

If your tendency is to finish turns by rotating hands and shoulders in

A

the direction of the turn (*B*), your uphill hand will slip behind you, out of sight. Push your uphill hand ahead of your body where you can see it. This will curb your tendency to rotate.

"Hug Your Girl" and Round Your Turn

by THOMAS EYNOLDS
Certified, U.S. Eastern Amateur Ski Association

Advanced skiers sometimes fail in making smooth precise turns because
they don't get their weight on the outside ski early enough in the turn.
One sure way to overcome this is to reach with your outside arm as
though you were going to hug your girl as you come over the fall line.
Make this movement fairly vigorously (sweep her off her feet!) and you
will get smoother, faster, and more precise turns.

156

Straighten Up to Ski Right

by JOHN PONNES
Certified, U.S. Eastern Amateur Ski Association

A common fault among parallel skiers is bending forward at the waist. Particularly if you are a little afraid of speed, you may tend to hunch your upper body forward in a very tense position at the end of a parallel turn.

To get rid of this bad habit, begin a series of parallel christies. Concentrate on finishing each turn with the entire length of your parka zipper in sight. After a few turns you may lose your upright body position and hunch over at the waist so that your zipper is partially hidden. You must stop immediately, correct your body position, and begin a new series of turns. In this manner you'll learn to ski upright and improve your parallel turns.

157

Don't Pose for the Camera!

by JON PUTNAM

Certified, U.S. Eastern Amateur Ski Association

Many skiers carry a mental image of an expert skier featured on a current ski poster or magazine cover. Trying to imitate the perfect body position in the photo, a skier will strike that pose (*A*) and then attempt to hold the position throughout an entire turn. Unfortunately, static positions on skis encourage a skier to sit back and make incomplete, skidded parallel turns.

Remember that a photograph represents a skier's body position for

A

B

only an instant. If you saw sequence photos of the skier on a poster, you would realize that his body was in continuous motion throughout the turn. Remember to keep your body flowing easily throughout each parallel turn—carving with your skis by driving your knees forward and adjusting your upper body position to maintain good balance (B). Fluid motion will help you ski more aggressively and improve your technique for steep slopes and challenging terrain.

Wind Up to Get Airborne

by STEVE BUTTS

Certified, Central Division, U.S. Ski Association

When attempting a gelandesprung, many skiers forget the down-up-down motion that they use in their regular skiing. The result is that rather than really taking off, they simply stand up slowly after leaving the edge of the bump and go into a slow tuck as they come in contact with the snow.

To get the flying sensation of a gelandesprung and to get height and distance, use these movements: (1) go down slowly as you approach the bump; (2) just before the crest, come up abruptly by springing with

your legs; (3) quickly bring your legs up to a tuck and hold them up.
You'll be amazed at how high you go and how long you soar. Remember
to straighten up just before you land on the snow and to absorb the
impact of landing with your knees.

Off the Fall Line for Expert Skiers

by DIXI NOHL

Certified, Austrian Association of Professional Ski Instructors and U.S. Eastern Amateur Ski Association

In previous chapters we discussed fall line practice procedures for beginners and intermediates; here are two for expert skiers:

Hop and Hit It

Turn your skis well into the slanted slope by thrusting the tails sharply downhill. At the same time, set your edges hard by bending your knees and pushing them into the hill. Plant your lower pole and quickly hop the tails uphill so that you begin to travel toward the fall line. Before the skis actually turn down the fall line, hit the tails again with a sharp thrust, an edge set, and a lowering of your upper body. You'll go up the hill again and can repeat the hop.

162

163

Weird Wedeln

This is where you can begin to put some speed into your off-the-fall-line skiing. Let your skis run into the slope at a fast speed, and before you begin to slow down, quickly raise your body to unweight your skis and change your edges. The moment you feel the skis start to turn, lean your upper body way out to the outside of the turn—that is, lean uphill. You can get away with this uphill lean, both because you are moving fast and because on the slanted slope you are momentarily counteracting the centrifugal forces of the turn, and in effect creating your own fall

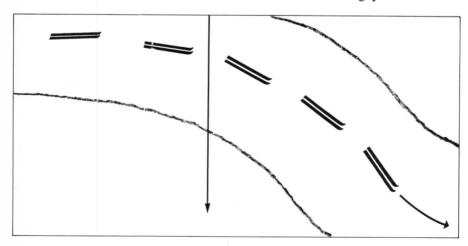

line. At the bottom of the slanted slope, raise your body and change the edges to get your skis moving up into the slope again. If the slope is narrow, this quick downhill turn becomes a kind of wedeln.

6. SPECIAL SNOW
AND TERRAIN CONDITIONS

The skier will encounter few difficulties in average snow conditions. By average is meant a snow surface reasonably firm, but not so firm that it is unyielding.

But conditions are rarely average. Fresh snow will fall, and if there is enough of it the skier will have to learn to cope with deep powder. It may rain or temperatures will rise above freezing, in which case the soft, wet snow poses its own special problems. And following these conditions it may freeze, and the skier must wrestle with the problems of ice. And invariably there are moguls—whole slopes of bumps—and there are special ways of dealing with these. Only when the skier can operate competently under all of these conditions can he be truly placed in the advanced class.

With the heavy traffic on today's slopes, the most commonly encountered snow condition difficulty is caused by the scraping away of snow. Ice may also form when temperatures drop below freezing following a day of warm temperatures (a frequent condition in spring). Ice may affect an entire slope; it may also be found in patches where shadows prevent the sun from thawing the snow. The first secret of ice skiing is equipment. Sharp ski edges and stiff boots that give lateral ankle support are essential to being able to hold and control skis—whether you're a beginner, an intermediate, or an expert.

The second secret of skiing on ice, at any ability level, is economy of movement: neither too much nor too little, neither too fast nor too slow. Just smooth, flowing, effortless, calm, icy elegance.

Cooling It on Ice

by GEORGES JOUBERT

For most beginners and intermediates who are doing snowplow or stem turns, this majestic cool must be applied during traverses across icy patches. Turns should be made on snow or rough, granular ice at the sides of the trails. More advanced skiers, to whom angulation has become instinctive, can carve or do short turns on ice as long as they keep their motions subtle and their skis in contact with the snow—er, ice.

The one constant in skiing any condition is keeping weight on the downhill ski in the traverse and on the outside ski in a turn. This is even more true on ice, where you must keep all your weight on one ski. An exercise you can do at home to prepare for skiing on ice is, standing in front of a mirror, to pretend that the inside edge of your foot is the edge of a ski. Put all of your weight on that "edge," then lift the other foot and press your weighted knee to the inside as you flex your leg. Not only will this give you the feeling of total weight on one ski, but it will force your body to angulate—you can see it in the mirror.

Traverse: Tilting the Ski

With all of your weight on the inside edge of the downhill ski, you should tilt the ski slightly toward the slope. This position (the right figure is correct) will hold you securely unless your edges are very dull. With too much edging (*left figure*), you will not be ready to turn when you have the opportunity.

Traverse: Angulation

With the hip well *into* the hill, the proper angulation (*top right figure*) directs the weight to the inside edge of the weighted, downhill ski. Naturally powerful people, who are not too supple, will hold on ice more easily than tall, flexible people. However, applying tense, muscular force (*top left figure*) makes progress tough.

Traverse: Holding Power

Standing fairly upright (*bottom right figure*) achieves maximum holding power from the skis. Experimenting with forward and back weight distribution in your stance, you'll find the balance point in your feet that holds you best. Too much knee flex (*bottom left figure*) hampers edge bite.

169

Turning: Correct

The right way to turn on ice is to suppress the up-and-down motion and to get the weight on the outside ski early, with the body in an angulated position (*see the fourth and fifth figures in the above illustration*). By shifting your weight smoothly from one to the other, you can keep your skis in contact with the snow (or ice) throughout the turn, giving you much more control.

Turning: Incorrect

In carving turns or making short wedeln turns, advanced skiers often find their skis sideslipping too far in an edge set (*see the fourth figure, above*), sometimes causing a fall. Their problem is too much up-and-down movement and too much abrupt action. They are slamming the skis onto their edges and using brute force to hold on.

Short Cuts on Ice

by WILLIAM S. MORRISON
Certified, U.S. Eastern Amateur Ski Association

Competent skiers often wonder why their strength or their style doesn't carry over from ideal snow conditions to ice. They fail to realize that skiing ice requires somewhat different movements. A platform or an edge set is still needed to maintain control on icy terrain, but it should be sharp and fast, and less powerful than you would use on soft snow. Fall

line skiing should look like illustration *A*, with the skis at an angle to the hill of approximately 45 degrees. Think of making a series of short, cutting turns on ice. On the other hand, if your edges make marks at a 90-degree angle, as in illustration *B*, you are overturning and sliding and working much too hard. This applies whether you are making stem or wedeln turns—your body movements must be precise to get the full benefit of your ski edges on the ice.

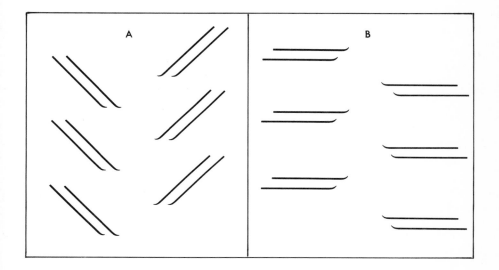

Anticipate Changing Snow Conditions

by WILLIAM STRALEY

Certified, Pacific Northwest Ski Instructors' Association

A new snowfall is always greeted with enthusiasm. However, you may experience some difficulty when the new snow becomes partially packed out by skiers or Sno-cats. Particularly when new snow has fallen on top of a hard icy surface, you may have difficulty maintaining your balance as you enter deep powder from icier areas. To avoid being pitched forward over your ski tips when you enter the powder snow, simply lower your center of gravity by sitting slightly down and back over the tails of your skis (see *A*).

A

B

Entering a hard-packed or icy area from deep powder, rise up slightly and lean forward in preparation for less resistant and faster snow conditions (see *B*).

Learn to anticipate changing snow conditions in your path by adjusting your body position. You'll soon become a more competent and confident skier.

Inside Edges for Ruts

by WILLIAM BRIGGS

Certified, U.S. Eastern Amateur Ski Association, Far West Instructors'
Association, Intermountain Ski Instructors' Association

When spring skiing during the morning and late afternoon, you'll find
that the mushy snow on the outruns of hills and trails has become
frozen. The result is hard, icy tracks that make it easy for you to catch
a ski edge and fall. To avoid catching that precarious outside edge, ski
the ruts by pressing both knees slightly inward and running on the inside
edges of your skis. Skiing slightly knock-kneed on your inside edges will
enable you to handle frozen ruts smoothly and without trouble.

How to Ski the Dips

by FRASER NOBLE
Certified, U.S. Eastern Amateur Ski Association

In spring, many skiers—even so-called experts—have difficulty negotiating a runout with ruts or a narrow catwalk. But the sharp dips can be fun as well as a test of your balance if you learn how to ski them well.

Straighten up full length, arms outstretched as you enter a dip. Then, allow the upward slope on the far side of the rut to bend your knees and lower your arms.

As you gain confidence through practicing this maneuver, you'll begin looking for the deepest section of a dip to ski through instead of aiming for the shallow sides.

177

Change Edges Positively

by JIM MCCONKEY
Certified, Canadian Ski Instructors' Alliance

The secret of skiing crud—slab or frozen surface that breaks through to soft snow underneath—is rapid, positive changing of your ski edges for each turn. Don't hesitate. Be positive.

To change the edges from one side to the other requires strong unweighting. Just how much unweighting or hopping you'll need depends on the resistance of the snow and the strength in your lower legs to steer the turn. The less the resistance and the stronger you are, the less unweighting you'll need to make the change from one set of edges to the other.

The main thing, though, is that there be no hesitation between one turn and the next. Keep the tips together and go quickly from one set of edges to the other. And remember: to learn how to ski deep snow, you must expect to have some falls. A good piece of advice is to "take 'er in the fall line and go till you clobber."

178

Skiing a Catwalk

by DIXI NOHL

Certified, Austrian Association of Professional Ski Instructors and U.S. Eastern Amateur Ski Association

For most skiers, a catwalk—a narrow trail shaped like a gunbarrel cut in half lengthwise—results in some embarrassingly awkward maneuvers on skis—muscular holding actions to prevent runaway skis and panic stops in the woods. For a few skiers, a steep, narrow trail or a catwalk is a real "psych-out" situation, causing terror and inability to coordinate. Actually, a catwalk can be mastered to the point where it is swinging fun, if not a groovy ride. Because catwalks can be dangerous, however, I advise anyone who has trouble with them to start learning to handle them as a beginner would and work up to the smoother, more elegant turns at your own pace. In any case, since catwalks can vary in shape, width, and snow conditions, it's good to know several methods of skiing them.

Banking Snowplow Turns

A catwalk can be an effective aid to snowplowing: running up and down the banks (as illustrated on the next page), the skis turn practically without effort. Let your skis run in a snowplow across the catwalk toward a high bank. As the tips start to go up the side of the bank, shift your weight to the outside ski. Almost immediately the skis will start to turn and run across the catwalk to go up the other bank. Don't be

179

afraid to let the skis get well up the bank before starting your turn; a positive weight shift will bring a fast change of direction.

Straight Crest Plow

Attempting to snowplow down the middle of a catwalk makes you feel as if you're doing a spread-eagle on a tightrope. The high banks on each side push back at your skis, restricting your ability to push the tails out to slow your speed. If you lose your braking power, the skis run away from you. To avoid this, let one ski run straight along the crest of the catwalk's bank (see above) while the other ski does the plowing in the trough. Due to the shape of the bank, this plowing ski actually runs uphill, adding braking power.

Double Bank Stem

Sometimes you can't slide along the bank because snow snags your ski tips, the bank is the wrong shape, or you simply become tired of sliding. Then you can use stem garlands to negotiate the catwalk. Let your skis slide up the side of the bank, and just before the tips reach the edge, open the skis in a snowplow. As they slide back down into the saucer, bring your skis together and thrust the tails downhill by bending your knees and ankles abruptly. This thrust will slow your speed and send you up the bank again. Repeat these garlands all the way down the catwalk.

High Side Slide

One easy way to get through a catwalk is to sideslip along the bank. Let the tips of your skis run up the bank until they practically go over the edge. Then sit back slightly to maintain your angle to the slope and put weight on the tails of your skis. From this position you can direct your sideslip and control your speed.

Garland Sidewinder

Catwalks crowded with skiers are difficult even for experts. One way around this situation is to aim for the side of the catwalk and use the bank to make wedel garlands. Let your skis slide up the side of the bank, and when the tips reach the edge, sit back slightly and push the tips down towards the fall line. Let them run down for an instant, and then bend forward again as you thrust the tails down to turn the skis back up the bank. If you need to slow your speed even more, use a pronounced edge set at the end of the tail thrust.

Midway Wedeln

The mark of a catwalk master is the ability to wedel down the middle of it in perfect control. On most catwalks the line down the center is fairly level and even. Use this to make very quick, very tight, linked parallel turns, controlling your speed with strong edge sets after each short turn. The trick of catwalk wedeln is to keep the skis close to the fall line. If they cut across the slope too much, the banked sides will grab the tips and pull you off line. Once you gain rhythm and momentum, you'll have it made.

Ski with Your Legs

by GUNTHER HOLWEG
Certified, Far West Ski Instructors' Association

If you're a good skier but lose all your style and control on steep trails or in moguls, try the following exercise.

On a novice or intermediate slope, remove the pole straps from your wrists and grasp the poles midway up the shaft. Place your skis about one foot apart.

Bend ankles and knees well forward so that you can plant your shortened ski poles while turning. Practice short parallel turns with aggressive pole plants for several runs. You'll discover that this exercise forces you to ski with your legs and to rely less on your upper body to turn. When you resume your poles at their normal length, simply straighten your upper body. Retain the same amount of ankle and knee flex on those steep trails and moguls.

Skiing the Steep

by ERNIE MCCULLOCH

You zing down an easy catwalk, make a right turn through a pleasant glade, and suddenly there is the edge of the earth—so steep you suck in some air and mumble, "What am I doing here?" There's no turning back; you have to get down. What to do?

This problem becomes all the more common as the season draws to a close and you've been doing quite a bit of skiing. That spring snow can be quite alluring. And it's easier to handle steep trails on spring corn and soft, mushy snow. Many beginning skiers and almost all intermediates inadvertently have found themselves on slopes too steep for their ability. Fortunately, there is always a way down from even the steepest slope. The main thing to remember is to keep your cool, go slowly, and maintain your confidence.

Now, for an expert or near-expert skier, a steep slope is what it's all about. For good skiers the essence of skiing steep slopes is alertness, aggressiveness, and rhythm. Be ready for anything, attack the slope, and try to maintain a smooth pace. Whatever your ability, try to use a variety of skids and turns—then you're really skiing steep.

Easy Forward Slide

An intermediate skier who is able to do a good stem christie will be able to do moving turns on most steep slopes. However, you should sideslip forward for a few yards before you try a turn in order to gain confidence, and also sideslip between turns to cover distance. Keep your feet separated for a secure stance, and look at the terrain in front of you —not down the mountain. When you see a likely spot for a turn (where the snow is good and there is a flat spot or a bump to help you), let your ski tails drift downhill to check forward momentum, and then edge your skis before you turn.

Quick "Pow" Plow

From the above forward sideslip and edging position, you are ready to do a stem christie turn. Stem your uphill ski as you plant your downhill pole well out to the side and down the hill. Steer your skis in a snowplow position to the fall line, keeping them well edged and putting most of your weight on the stemmed ski. As you cross the fall line, pick up your inside ski and bring it parallel to the other one, keeping it separated to aid your balance.

Remember that you are on a steeper slope and will have more speed than usual, so all of your movements should also be quicker. Bring those skis together without hesitation as you move around the fall line. Then edge your skis and let the tails drift downhill to slow your speed.

Classic Control

For this turn, with the skis parallel, the edges are set or turned into the hill with a strong down motion of the knees. At the same time, the pole is planted well down the hill, producing an angulated position of the body (note the second and fifth figures). As you extend your body, move the unweighted skis laterally and toward the fall line, then move your weight to the outside ski and steer across the fall line. Check your speed with another pronounced edge set and continue turning.

Compression Turn

This is like the French avalement turn, which is much faster than the classic control. At the end of a turn, lower your hips and plant your downhill pole out to the side. The skis will shoot out in front of you, and it is here that you use strong steering action with your knees to turn the skis across the fall line. The pole can be kept in the snow as an aid to balance almost to the point where you are facing down the fall line.

Control your speed by the radius of your turn: the narrower the arc, the slower your speed. In this type of turn, it can be difficult to slow down on a steep slope once you are moving fast, so try to keep your arcs under control.

Walking Down

It may seem ignominious to shoulder your skis and walk down, but sometimes this is the wisest choice for beginners. Tie your skis together securely with the runaway straps and put them over one shoulder with the tips pointing down. Use the poles in your opposite hand as a walking support. Dig your heels in as you go down to keep a secure footing, and walk on the sides of the trail so you won't leave deep holes that may catch other skiers' skis.

Turn on a Kick Turn

If you can do a forward sideslip on an intermediate hill, you can probably manage it on steeper slopes as well (see the instructions for an easy forward slide, p. 188). When you reach the edge of the trail or a bump that will give you a platform, stop for a kick turn. Edge your uphill ski very securely, and with both poles in the snow kick the down-hill ski up and forward and quickly swing it around to face in the op-posite direction. Place it securely in the snow, and test its ability to hold your weight. When it is firm, lift your uphill ski and swing it around. Continue sideslipping until you can make another kick turn.

One word of caution: Never try to learn a kick turn on the slope. Practice it on the flat until you feel confident with it; then adapt it to the hill. Everyone should learn to do this important maneuver.

Pivot Around Your Pole

This drawing indicates the skier's actual position on the slope during the stem christie turn. Note that he pivots around the ski pole. In the illustration at right he is shown moving to the side in order clearly to reveal the positions of his skis and body.

Reach Downhill

by ROBERT LEONARD
Certified, Far West Ski Instructors' Association

The key to building your confidence for handling steep terrain is in knowing how to control your speed. Speed is controlled on steep terrain by doing short radius turns linked down the fall line.

The easiest way to cut short radius arcs on a steep hill is to reach downhill with your pole before the turn, planting it almost in a line with your boots. This vigorous reaching out with the downhill arm will start your shoulders and torso turning downhill in a pre-turn position. With the body in this position, the skis can be twisted in the direction of the turn when they are unweighted.

A short radius turn executed in this manner will make it easier for you to master steep slopes and narrow trails—under control.

Jump High for a Quick Turn

by DENNIS WELLS

Certified, Central Division, U.S. Ski Association

Here's a quick way to turn around from a standstill and a nervy way to
turn around on steep slopes. Be sure you've got a good platform under
your skis, and then sink down quick and hard as you plant both poles.
Spring your body up, pushing from the poles and bringing your feet up
under you. When you have reached the highest point of your jump (it
may take you a few practice jumps to determine this), make your body
rigid so that it can be swung around your downhill pole as one unit. The
key to the success of your turn occurs right here: as you are pivoting
around this downhill pole, place all of your weight directly on it and
bring the uphill pole around. Complete the turn by sinking in your knees
as you land. You'll need plenty of arm strength for this maneuver as well
as lots of practice, but keep trying and you'll soon jump high and around.

How to Do a Fast Fall-Out

by K. McLaughlin

Certified, Canadian Ski Instructors' Alliance

An occasional fall when skiing may be a good sign. It can mean that you are pushing the limits of your ability, not resting on a plateau. Good skiers, of course, do fall now and then. A common type of fall among parallel skiers occurs in soft snow because of poor edging. The fall is usually toward the downhill, and while it is awkward, it's rarely dangerous.

If you are a reasonably agile person, there's an easy and quick way to exit from this kind of fall. I call it *the flip* or *the fall-out*. First, as always the fall should be relaxed. As you fall downhill, react like a tumbler. Tuck your head down, draw the knees in and kick your feet and skis up and over. Use the momentum of the fall to keep yourself rolling over in a continuous motion. You'll quickly tumble back onto your skis, ready to continue on down the hill.

Thrust in Slush

by Dixi Nohl
Certified, Austrian Association of Professional Ski Instructors and U.S. Eastern Amateur Ski Association

When the hot spring sun softens the snow and turns it into deep slush, many skiers use a series of jump turns in the heavy snow. Because jump turns require a lot of energy and added leg work, you may find yourself quite overheated and tired before the end of the day. In addition, jump turns cause your skis to sink deeper in the snow when you land, making the next turns more difficult. Instead of jumping, make turns close to the fall line with a minimum of unweighting, simply thrusting the tails of your skis toward the outside of the turn. With each thrust, a platform of snow will build up under your skis to control speed. At the same time, the sticky, wet snow will check your speed, making it unnecessary to turn far out of the fall line and still maintain control.

The "Scoot Foot"

by John McHale

In very advanced skiing and racing today, there's a great deal less bouncing from one set of edges to the other, and much more emphasis on keeping the skis in contact with the snow at all times. Unweighting is hardly perceptible. Rather, the skier, using advanced equipment, initiates the turn by anticipating its direction with the upper body, thrusts the feet forward to flatten his skis and then exerts pressure on the inside edges to turn. I call this kind of turn the *scoot foot*.

To visualize the scoot foot, think of yourself as sitting on the edge of a chair, with your shoulders facing more or less downhill. To turn, scoot

both feet forward and turn them downhill. Then scoot your feet back under the chair to where they started: you are now in the middle of the turn and proceeding into the new traverse position.

Scoot foot produces a silky, smooth style of wedeln. It's great over moguls because your skis tend to stay in contact with the snow. It's also excellent for deep snow because the scoot seems to make the skis slice through the snow laterally.

Extend on Moguls to Steer Your Skis

by JONATHAN JENKINS
Examiner, Canadian Ski Instructors' Alliance

Skiers who have difficulty skiing bumpy terrain often compound their problems by becoming tense.

Instead of tightening up, you should relax and let your legs and ankles act as shock absorbers.

After crossing a mogul crest in a compressed position (to absorb the rising terrain), extend your legs to keep the skis in contact with the down side of the bump; let your body weight move forward over the feet again. With skis in contact with the snow, you can steer a precise turn. Failure to extend legs as the terrain steepens will cause you to lose control and make it impossible to compress again on the next bump.

204

The Correct Pole Plant for Moguls

by RUEDI WYRSCH

Certified, Swiss National Ski School and U.S. Eastern Amateur Ski Association

On moguls, *when* you turn is often as important as *how*. If you turn too late, your ski tips will hang up in a trough just beyond the bump; turn too early and the tails will catch behind you. But if your timing is perfect, you can ski right up on the mogul and swivel both skis in a turn so that neither tips nor tails touch the snow surface.

The easiest way to set up proper timing for a swivel turn is with a pole plant made precisely on the highest line of a mogul. A pole plant exactly on target (see line) sets up the timing so that each turn begins precisely at the moment when only the center of your skis touch the snow surface and your skis can swivel freely on top of the bump. Concentrate on a bull's-eye pole plant and you'll soon find yourself making easy rhythmical turns on terrain you once avoided.

Down-Unweight for Better Control

by Othmar Schneider

Keeping your skis on the snow while turning on moguls gives you greater control. To unweight the skis (see the top illustration, opposite page), your body must be in a low crouch when you reach the top of the bump. The secret in doing this is to start sinking down before your reach the top. I tuck my legs when my ski tips are about four inches from the crest of the bump, but exactly when and where you sink down depends on your speed, the size of the bump, and the steepness of the hill. It takes practice to meld these factors into a practical formula.

As you come down the side of the bump, straighten up to prepare for the next turn. Keep looking ahead for suitable bumps and a good line down the slope.

Using up-unweighting (bottom illustration, opposite page), skiers fly over bumps as if out of control, riding over long stretches of bumps in between long, wide turns. This is all right if the intention is to do airborne turns. The turn illustrated here was done on the same mogul as the previous turn, but note how my body came up off the bump after unweighting with an up motion. I flew out much farther than in the down-unweighted turn, and upon landing I had to regain control.

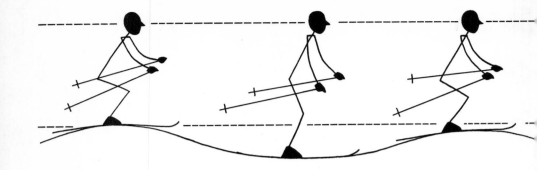

Keep a Level Head

by GREGORY K. LEE
Certified, Rocky Mountain Ski Instructors' Association

Many skiers develop a fear of skiing through moguls because their skis lose contact with the snow and they are tossed in the air from one bump to the next. The best way to ski moguls in control is to keep the entire length of your skis in contact with the snow.

Practice skiing across a series of tightly spaced moguls, keeping the upper body fairly upright, and absorb the bumps in the terrain with your legs. Have a mental image of your head moving in a straight line across a slope while your legs coil and extend in bumps to keep your skis in touch with the snow. When you approach a mogul, increase ankle and knee bend, reaching a low position on the mogul crest. Gradually extend your legs in the depressions between bumps.

After improving your body position and timing by traversing through moguls, apply what you've learned to turning—compressing the legs to begin each turn and extending the lower body to control the final arc.

Control Your Speed on Icy Moguls

by BRUCE SIMPSON
Certified, Canadian Ski Instructors' Alliance

Skiing icy moguls, the track you choose is as important as your ability to ski. When you reach the top of an icy mogul field, first check the rough ice or snowy patches on the uphill side of each mogul. Let your skis slide forward and sideways without edging toward one of these patches. Upon reaching the loose snow, sink down sharply, setting the edges of your skis, and plant your lower ski pole. As a result of your sudden down motion and edge set, your skis should come almost to a complete stop. Next, relax and let your skis slide forward, twisting them toward another bump in a forward sideslip. Repeat the same, sharp sinking motion and edge set before each turn, absorbing this sharp edge set with well-flexed legs.

Learning to control your speed and direction in icy conditions will help you to learn good edge control and become a better all-around skier. You'll learn to enjoy those moguled ski trails, even on icy days.

The Banked Turn

by CORKY FOWLER

The most efficient way to ski deep snow is to consider the snow as having the same effect on your skis as water does on water skis. That is, you're dealing with a soft pliable surface that the skis can sink into. A water skier turns by banking. A snow skier can do the same in deep snow.

Starting in the fall line, the demonstrator first gathers enough speed to get the skis planing near the surface of the soft snow. The turn is started by simply edging the skis in the direction of the desired turn. As the skis meet the resistance of snow on the bottoms, the skier merely starts leaning in the turning direction. His weight rests against the bottoms of the skis as the turn progressively increases the resistance of the snow and causes the skis to turn even more sharply.

To start the next turn, the skier releases the pressure of the leg slightly (retracts), causing the resistance against the snow to end momentarily. The knees move laterally to change the edges and simultaneously start leaning or banking with the upper body in the new direction.

Banking turns in soft snow is fun, especially at high speed. You develop tremendous centrifugal force at the apex of the turn, like riding a roller coaster.

Putting a Ski On in Deep Snow

by BARBARA RUEGG

Certified, U.S. Eastern Amateur Ski Association

Getting back into your binding in very deep powder can be a frustrating and fatiguing experience. There is usually no firm surface on which to place the ski. Moreover, the loose snow accumulates in the binding— a circumstance that you must prevent with step-in models, because they will not operate if snow is caked between your boot sole and ski.

The problems of a ski replacement in deep powder can be overcome if you employ the following procedure. Take the detached ski and set its midpoint across the toe of the opposite boot. Resting your weight on one ski pole, take the other pole and hook its basket onto the tip of the loose ski. This ski is now set on a relatively solid platform consisting of the toe of your boot and the basket of your pole, which you can pull on to steady the tip of the ski. Even more important, your ski is elevated slightly so that the surrounding snow can't fall on the binding area. After checking to see that snow is not caked on the sole of your boot, center it carefully on the binding. Steady the ski tip by using the pole basket, then step forward and down into the heel unit. You're back on the ski.

Wait for "the Floating Sensation"

by WALLACE A. DAY

The basic rules for skiing powder include skiing with legs close together and weighting skis evenly. In addition, a simple adjustment in timing will enable you to ski deep snow with greater ease.

If you ski in powder by down-unweighting your skis, you will finish each turn in an extended position. Then, sink down and wait for the floating sensation caused by your skis rising upward toward the snow surface. Next, rise up slowly to turn. You'll find that slowing down your timing between turns to allow your skis to float upward makes turning in deep snow much easier. Soon you'll be linking a dozen or more rhythmical turns in the fall line.

Of course, flexible skis are necessary. They must bend easily when weighted, and snap back to their original shape and rise to the surface when unweighted.

The "Sitting Back" Myth

by JUNIOR BOUNOUS
Certified, Rocky Mountain Ski Instructors' Association

The easiest advice given to skiers in deep powder is "to sit back." But the most common fault of a skier in deep powder is sitting back incorrectly or too far. The trick in deep snow is to get an even distribution of weight on the balls and heels of your feet. This is your best assurance that you'll not apply too much pressure to the tips (which will drive into the snow) or too much on the tails (which will prevent you from pushing them side to side).

How do you obtain this kind of equal pressure distribution? The answer is a very moderate sitting position, but with the knees well bent. Sitting back without bending the knees will create unequal weight distribution and result in frequent falls. A supple, bent knee is your best means of assuring even pressure distribution over the ski—the only way to ski deep powder.

"Step Off a Tack" in Heavy Snow

by LYNDA GREDA

Certified, Canadian Ski Instructors' Alliance

Heavy spring snow often causes a radical change in skiing style from lithe, supple swinging to vigorous up-unweighting. Every time the skier lands, he is thrown off balance.

When you face these conditions, instead of thinking about the snow, conjure a mental image of stepping on a tack in your bare feet. Your immediate reaction will be to soften the effects of your landing by bending your knees, exactly the technique you need in heavy spring snow. You'll find that you can keep your balance better and also make smoother, more graceful turns.

Be a "Sleeping Beauty"

by BARBARA WICKS

Certified, U.S. Eastern Amateur Ski Association

On a warm spring day, many skiers enjoy a short nap or sun bath, using their skis and poles to lean on, as shown below. Choose a site well to the side of ski trails and out of the path of skiers moving downhill. Then, simply place both ski poles several feet apart in the snow, with each pole strap looped over the opposite pole grip. Rest the tips of both skis, running surface up, on the pole straps between the grips. With poles tipped just slightly toward your skis, the weight of your body will be easily supported by your ski equipment.

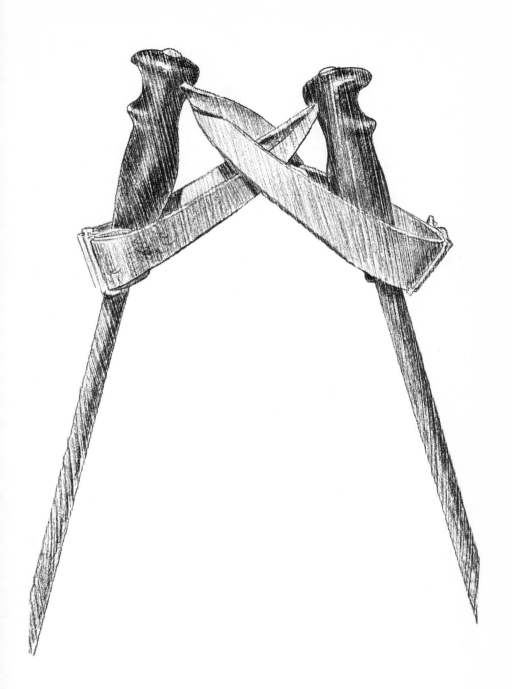

In Spring, Ski by the Clock

by JOHN FRY

Skiers who extract the most pleasure from a day of spring skiing do so as a result of planning, not luck. Before you start up the mountain in the morning, give careful consideration to the fact that the slopes will face the sun at different times of the day. Keep in mind that ideal spring snow sets up with about an inch of soft corn on top of a firm surface. When the sun rises in the morning after a cold night, all slopes will be frozen hard. Look on the mountains or at the area trail map for slopes facing east. These are the trails that will get the earliest sun and where the top layer will lose its icy surface first. It's where you will find the best conditions when the lifts open. As the sun mounts higher and the day gets warmer, the east-facing slopes become slushy and heavy. This is the time to start using different lifts, moving counterclockwise around the mountain to find snow surfaces that have softened enough to offer ideal skiing but are not yet too soft. By late afternoon, you may find it preferable to move back to an east-facing slope: if the air temperature is cold enough, the sun will now hit such slopes at an oblique angle and they may firm up enough to offer a good skiing surface again.

Smart scrutiny of weather and terrain can improve your day of skiing immeasurably.

7. SKI RACING AND NASTAR

If you enjoy competition, skiing is the sport that can provide it—no matter how seriously you want to take it or how old you are. The best way to obtain this competition for the recreational skier is enter sanctioned standard races.

In 1968, *Ski Magazine* introduced the National Standard Ski Race (*NASTAR*) to a limited number of ski areas. The idea behind NASTAR is that you can ski down an open, flagged giant slalom course on an easy hill on any day of the winter under any conditions and still wind up with a performance time comparable to that of another skier on a different day. It does not matter if you skied a NASTAR course in Vermont and the other fellow did it in Colorado. As with golf, NASTAR awards you a handicap rating, uniform for all skiers.

Many ski areas around the country have converted their standard races to the NASTAR system. If you enter one of these races, your performance will be compared with that of the local pro whose time has been corrected to the national standard. Your goal: to narrow the time gap between yourself and the pacesetter and thereby lower your handicap. Depending on whether you're under or over the age of 40, a male skier must come within 10 or 20 percent and women within 15 or 25 percent of the national standard time to win a gold pin. Silver and bronze pins are awarded at other percentage levels. The percent by which each skier is slower than the national standard is also computed regardless of any award won, and this percent becomes the skier's handicap. A wallet-sized NASTAR handicap card is sent to every competitor, showing the amount of his handicap. If a skier enters a subsequent NASTAR event and achieves a lower handicap, he will be issued a new card showing his revised handicap.

A skier's handicap can be employed in different ways, ranging from conversational one-upmanship to a practical way of handicapping a challenge race among recreational skiers of different abilities. Such a competition would be different from today's conventional ski race, in which the actual or lowest "gross" time determines the winner. Rather, in a handicapped race, the "net" time would count, as net scores count in golf. In effect, people would ski down a course and then correct their actual times by the amount of their NASTAR handicaps to yield a net time. That is, if the pacesetter's nationally corrected time, for instance, is 36 seconds, and you make your run in 44 seconds, the difference is 8 seconds, or 25 percent slower than the national standard. Thus your handicap becomes 25 and you receive a silver pin. A person may enter as many NASTAR races as possible in order to try to lower his handicap.

How to Go for NASTAR Gold

by ROGER STAUB

With many resorts from coast to coast taking part in the National Standard Ski Race program, the opportunity to race now faces the average recreational skier. Judging from the past, the average skier, when he's done, will ask, "Now how did my buddy make such good time on the course when he didn't look all that fast?" Your buddy may

know a little about racing; he may know, for starters, that a skier who travels a "long path" is going to get beaten by a skier who travels no faster but takes a "short path." The two composite pictures here show the secret of making the "short path," the first thing a neophyte racer must learn. In the composite on page 221, I demonstrate the "short path": right after each gate, you can see me making a "skate-up," or skating step. This gives me a "high line" and gives me a better angle

at the upcoming gate. Coming into each gate, I am therefore able to cut quite close to the gate, nearly brushing it with my back. I get a tight, short turn without having to jam my skis into the snow and killing my speed. The tight, round turn made possible by the skating step is the key to winning your NASTAR or any other race. In the composite above, you see what happens when I don't "skate up." I have to make a sharper turn at each gate and tend to overshoot. In the first gate I overshoot just a little, in the second a little more, and by the third gate, still trying to keep my speed up, I have overshot to the point that I am almost off the course. By comparing my path (heavy line) with the path I had taken through the gates in the first picture (dotted line), you can see that not only am I overshooting and skidding, but I am traveling a longer and longer path, losing precious time with every turn I make. So, skate up. It's the secret.

Rocket Starts

by SCOT LITKE
Certified, U.S. Eastern Amateur Ski Association

Some races are actually won right at the starting gate; indeed, expert racers often jump through the starting gate to gain valuable seconds. But for junior races and NASTAR events, practicing a more basic starting technique from a level platform will gain rewards.

Before you are ready to race, listen to the countdown on other racers to learn the cadence of the starter's count; an alert anticipation can save seconds at the top of the course. When it's your turn, step into the start and plant poles securely in the snow in front of the gate to make a firm launch pad. Prepare for an explosive start by coiling your body like a spring. With the last signal of the countdown, rock forward, weighting your ski poles and use arm, shoulder, stomach, and leg muscles to explode out of the gate. Feet should snap through the starting gate last. Don't overskate or make other unnecessary motions in an attempt to gain speed once you are out of the gate: off-balance starts often result in spills at the first gate. Turn early for the first gate. Then concentrate on building up rhythm and following a good line through the course.

Tip Down to Step Up

by PETER PALMER
Certified, U.S. Eastern Amateur Ski Association

In NASTAR and other standard races, you will frequently encounter gates where you can gain speed through the course by stepping uphill into a new and faster line. Many skiers are unable to step uphill because they bank their turns or lean uphill and weight the uphill ski. It is impossible to step higher onto the uphill ski if your weight is already on it (*A*).

Approaching a gate where you must step uphill to establish a good line, be sure to tip your lower shoulder downhill so that you can weight the downhill ski. Then quickly step the opposite ski higher uphill into a new and faster line toward the next gate (*B*).

Don't Duck, Reach Downhill

by ANDY MCMASTER

To win a NASTAR gold medal, you'll need to choose a fast line and stick to it. Often skiers lose their line by ducking the inside shoulder under the inside pole of each gate. This starts a chain of events in which the hips are released to the outside of the turn and the ski edges begin slipping and skidding out of the chosen line. The trick is to reach down and out with the outside arm in each turn. If you keep the outside arm low at all times, shoulders and hips will line up properly to hold your skis on edge and ride the fastest, straightest line through the course.

226

"See" a Second Finish

by JOHN ANTHONY SMITH
Certified, U.S. Eastern Amateur Ski Association

Many NASTAR entrants are able to zip through the beginning and middle sections of the course with ease, only to spin out of the course or fall just before the finish. This is usually the result of concentrating heavily on the harder sections of the course and then relaxing as the last gates and finish line loom into sight.

To avoid last-minute lapses in concentration, imagine a finish line somewhat beyond the actual finish of the race. Combat the tendency to relax prematurely by skiing hard through the timing mechanisms at the actual finish and right on through the imaginary gate.

The Racer's Step

by JOHN FRY

Here's a turn that will improve your NASTAR score by several points.

The racing step is the functioning turn of the giant slalom. The skier's aim is to go directly and on as short a line as possible from one gate to the next. Normally, this does not leave a great deal of room to make a turn. One option is to make an uphill checking turn to get high enough on the gate, but this is a sure way to lose speed. The solution is the step turn, which not only gets you up the hill and on a line to make the turn on the outside ski, but the act of pushing off the downhill ski maintains and increases speed.

The sequence illustrated here shows how it's done. The skier traverses across the hill, pushes off the downhill ski to accelerate, and steps on the uphill ski. Finally, he puts it on edge and starts the turn.

The step turn's value is not limited to racing. For any skier wishing to make a big stride forward in skiing, it's an important turn to learn because it teaches you how to "go outside"—that is, to get on the outside ski of the turn early and make it carve on the snow.

"Hopped-Up" Side Jumps

by H. H. Merrifield

At the starting gate, ski racers use exercises to loosen up tense muscles before starting down a racecourse. Here's a warm-up exercise you can perform on any piece of flat terrain to relax your muscles and improve your recreational racing as well as your skiing.

Standing on a level area with skis parallel, jump the tails of both skis simultaneously to one side without changing the location of your ski tips. Several more hops in the same direction will bring you halfway around a circle. Return to your starting point by hopping in the opposite direction. Finish with a series of jumps to the left and right. Besides stimulating your circulation and relaxing your muscles, this exercise will teach you simultaneous weighting and unweighting of your skis.

High or Low Crouch

by BILLY KIDD

Speed and terrain should dictate the proper height for your tuck. On a flat, easy run with absolutely no bumps, try to keep your chest as low as possible (*A*). When your chest is hitting against your knees, you will attain an aerodynamically fast body position.

However, when you reach little bumps, raise your chest slightly, and at the same time move your hips up, too, so that your back is parallel to your skis (*B*). This higher position promotes stability without increasing wind resistance against your chest and provides clearance for the knees to move up and down over the bumps underneath your chest. If your tuck is too low through rough terrain, a bump may suddenly push your knees and chest up in the air. If you catch the wind at a very high speed, it may flip you over backwards. A higher hip and chest position will give your knees more room to work in the bumps without hitting your chest.

A

B

A

Don't Clip the Pole

by BILLY KIDD

You could be standing up too straight and leaning toward the inside of the turn when you hit the pole with your shoulder. In slalom I brush the pole and let it slide by on my forearm: besides my arm, the part of my body closest to the pole is my thigh (*A*). As soon as my kneecap clears the pole, the pole brushes against my thigh. I know I'm running good slalom when both my arms and the outsides of my thighs get sore from hitting the poles.

If just the tops of my shoulders hit the poles, then I know that I'm leaning toward the inside of the turn too much and my skis are getting too far from the pole (*B*). To correct this, I try to exaggerate leaning my upper body farther away from the hill and pressing my knees into the hill. This helps me become more stable and ski closer to the poles.

232

B

Schwoomp! The Racer's Stop

by OTHMAR SCHNEIDER

One thing every budding downhill racer learns—as much for fun as necessity—is how to stop quickly while running a course. Because this stop sends up a big rooster tail of snow, it is used to throw snow over spectators (usually pretty girls), photographers, coaches, or teammates. Out of necessity, of course, racers use this stop in emergencies.

Even while practicing downhill, a racer can get up to speeds of fifty or sixty miles an hour. A stop from this pace has to be somewhat violent, as well as rapid. From a crouch position the racer straightens his body, thereby unweighting the skis, and at the same time throws the skis sideways to the fall line. This produces a sideslip, from which he edges his skis more and more to slow his speed until he can finally stop. During the sideslip his body leans into the hill for balance, and at the moment of stopping he sinks rapidly and edges hard, producing the sound *schwoomp*. At the moment of stopping, he usually angulates downhill and reaches out with his pole for stability.

While this stop has been used by racers for years, it is something that almost any strong, competent parallel skier can learn.

234

Hands Out in Front

by Arno Erath

Associate Certification, Far West Ski Instructors' Association

One of the most common faults of young racers and people first taking up slalom is that they allow their arms to extend outward too much or to drop back going through the course. The result is all too obvious—a frequent tendency to catch slalom poles and fall backwards.

To obtain the correct arm position for slalom, practice going through a course without your ski poles. In the effort to drive yourself close to the inside pole of each gate and stay in balance, you'll find that both arms will be thrown forward. This is a natural position, and one which will best assure you that your arms and pole won't become entangled with the flags. It's also good exercise for sharpening your balance and timing in slalom.

Racing Under Ice Conditions

by BILLY KIDD

On ice, it is most important to be able to turn your skis with your ankles and knees while keeping your hips completely quiet and your upper body straight over the center of your skis. One exercise in particular helped me learn to ski ice well: I used to practice it on the large, high moguls that formed each year on the National at Stowe, Vermont.

On each large mogul, I made three or four turns, as illustrated in the drawing above. Hitting my edges hard when I reached the crest of the mogul, I then hopped my skis quickly in the opposite direction and landed on the other side of the bump. Then I hit my edges again to make another hop, and so on. After learning to turn the skis quickly using just ankles and knees, I was then able to ski on ice better.

When you practice this exercise, you'll discover that you cannot turn quickly on the mogul if you use your hips and upper body to turn. You must learn to press your knees into the hill to set your edges and then quickly hop over the mogul crest to land on the other side. Also, remember to keep your hands out in front of your body while turning.

8. ACROBATICS

The essence of acrobatics for the ordinary skier (as opposed to someone who does them professionally at ski shows and exhibitions) is to vary the routine of skiing. It is a well-known fact that intermittent practice of a given skill is more efficient than massive doses of practice. In other words, it is practical to introduce a few acrobatic maneuvers to the skier who is classed as intermediate and better. The experience of the teachers who have tried it, and the skiers who have tried it, is that the introduction of the element of "having a ball" pays off.

For one thing, most American skiers are quite technique-conscious. They have, whether they realize it or not, considerable concentration on doing things right. This is fine. But it can also lead to stiff and un-relaxed skiing. This is where acrobatics comes in. The simple introduction of something different, something quite useless in itself, something on which nothing depends and which means little if not successful—this is the ideal "relaxation."

The skier who tries something, even a royal christie (see page 252), is likely to find that after a few successful or unsuccessful turns, it doesn't matter which, he will suddenly start skiing better when he returns to his "standard" turns. This is, of course, a well-known gambit: one "just for fun" interlude is used in many kinds of teaching, particularly in the teaching of physical skills. Something about the complete lack of pressure in attempting an acrobatic turn—you have never tried it, so don't worry about not making it—is carried over into your next turn.

This is not to say that more specific results can't be had from acrobatics. The very act of attempting to do something a bit out of the ordinary will call forth additional skill at balancing, timing, and edge control—the skills that are the "secret" of expert skiers.

Learn Acrobatics with Ease

by PAUL PFOSI
Certified, Swiss National Ski School and U.S. Eastern Amateur Ski Association

Today many ski schools utilize short skis in beginner programs. However, the benefits of short skis should by no means be restricted to beginners. Shorter lengths can be used effectively by advanced skiers to learn acrobatic maneuvers.

Rent a pair of skis, three to four feet long. You'll discover that the short, lighter skis will help you learn many acrobatic maneuvers. For instance, begin with a crossover. Practice this trick as illustrated. From a straight running position, pick up one ski and cross it forward over the opposite ski. Set the crossed ski down and transfer your weight to it before swinging the other ski backwards in the air to cross behind you. Repeat in a series of crossovers on down the ski slope.

The Reverse Jump Turn

by BRUCE GAVETTE
Certified, U.S. Eastern Amateur Ski Association

Here's a trick you can practice on grassy terrain, or even on a rug indoors (see following pages), so you'll be able to perform it with ease as soon as the snow flies. Even if you wait until winter to try this jump on snow, you'll discover that it's a real crowd pleaser, and just a little more difficult than a forward jump turn.

On snow, remove the pole straps and ski across a shallow hill in a very slow traverse. Sink down and plant the poles close together on the downhill side of your ski tips. With legs bent, rise up high on your poles and rotate the lower part of your body backward around the poles. Because you must jump backward out of a forward traverse, you will need a very strong double pole plant to break your forward momentum. Then you must be sure to jump high enough, at least two feet off the snow, so you have enough time to turn your lower body and twist your skis around in a new direction.

241

The fall warm-up for the reverse jump: On level ground, place hands on top of pole grips, letting straps dangle. Take several steps forward, sink down and plant both ski poles close to and slightly ahead of your feet.

Rise up off the ground, using arms and ski poles to support your body weight.

Draw feet and knees up tight, while pivoting backward around your poles. Practice gaining height off the ground.

After turning 180 degrees, lower legs to land below poles, absorbing the shock with your knees.

The Super Skip

by ARTHUR FURRER

This is a trick done in place: Start with both skis pointed forward, then swing one ski so that the tip points back toward the tail of the other, on the outside (*first figure*). As the ski lands (*second figure*), put your weight on it, and pull the other ski off the snow with the aid of one pole. Now bend the knee with the weight on it, spring into the air with the aid of the second pole, and pull the first pole as both skis swing around in the direction of the arrow (*third figure*) to face the original direction (*lower figure*). Note that the second ski must pass under the first ski.

The Bunny Hop

by ARTHUR FURRER

To do this one, you start out in a tip stand, with poles well forward (*above left*). Then (*center figure*), move forward on the poles, retract the ski tips from the snow, and hop them toward the poles, letting the tips sink in the snow again (*third figure*). Quickly repeated, this makes the skier appear to be a big bunny hopping along the slope.

The Outrigger Turn

by Tom Mulkern
Certified, U.S. Eastern Amateur Ski Association

At the end of the season, people are often anxious to try something new on skis. For a change of pace, try the outrigger turn.

From a traverse, begin turning by flattening both skis. Sink down into a very low crouch and direct your weight over the inside ski of the turn. When you are in a squat, with your weight far forward toward the tip of the inside ski, extend the outside leg so that the outside ski tip crosses the fall line and points in the opposite direction of the turn to form the outrigger. Be sure to tuck the knee over the inside ski tightly under your chest to get maximum support during the turn. Lean forward to apply

pressure on the tip of the inside ski and tip the ski slightly on the inside edge to turn out of the fall line. Swing the outside arm around in the direction of the turn in a follow-through motion. The outrigger ski can be drawn up parallel when the turn is complete.

The Javelin Wedeln

by ARTHUR FURRER

The javelin that I use is a fast-twisting ski, especially good for the short, little one-ski turns shown here. Begin by going into a regular wedeln, then pick up one ski (*top right*), cross the leg over the knee of the other leg (*center figure*), and let it all float while you continue to wedel down the slope on one ski. This takes good edge control. In the changeover between left and right turns, the ski must go flat, and then edge quickly to get the turn going.

The Royal Christie

by JOSE HANFF

Many skiers want to learn such acrobatic tricks as the royal christie but lack a logical sequence of steps to learn acrobatics. As with any other maneuver on skis, exercises are helpful in directing your progress toward the final goal.

The best way to learn edge control for a royal christie is to practice uphill christies on one ski. Using the right ski, practice turning to the right, and vice versa. From a traverse, lean your upper body slightly uphill in the direction of the turn, pressing your knee downhill to release the edge of the ski in a forward sideslip. Use your leg muscles and foot to steer the ski uphill. To improve your balance, spread your arms wide to either side. When you gain confidence, increase the steepness of your traverses.

The Tip Roll

by DIXI NOHL

*Certified, Austrian Association of Professional Ski Instructors and U.S.
Eastern Amateur Ski Association*

To do a tip roll the easy way, place both ski-pole grips underneath your

armpits, with the pole baskets in the snow about two feet below your
skis. Place the pole under your uphill arm, even with your ski boot, and
the other pole basket just slightly behind it. From this position, hop up
into the air, throwing the entire weight of your body onto your ski poles.
With the tips of your skis on the snow, swing your feet and the tails of

251

your skis around 180 degrees. When you've mastered this easy tip roll, you can try the real thing by placing your hands on top of your pole grips to turn. This tip roll is more difficult because you will need more strength in your arms to support the weight of your body and a higher spring in the air to turn your skis around.

9. TIPS TO THE PARENTS

If you started to ski late in life, you are bound to reflect on the ease with which children ski. They seem to be fearless and relaxed. They take the most hair-raising tumbles in stride. And they ski so fast. Inevitably you conclude that your own children should have a similar good start. Such intentions are noble and commendable, but before you begin you might contrast their experience with yours when you started out.

A ski school class of adults start out by lining up raggedly like a squad of recruits. The instructor talks, they listen. If he is a good one, he talks entertainingly. He demonstrates, they watch. One at a time his pupils take their turns; the instructor shouts exhortations and retrieves the fallen while the others maintain their formation. An altogether purposeful and orderly procedure.

All this may be slow, but by the end of the lesson weak knees are trembling, shins are aching, and muscles protesting. More to the point, adults must first understand what they are attempting to do before they try it. By the end of their first lesson, most will be able to do a snowplow, perhaps turn a little.

Children won't put up with this. The lecture amusing to adults is to them seemingly endless and mostly incomprehensible. Standing still in the cold is a form of torture, and looking awkward in front of an adult is an embarrassment. The child leaves for the bathroom, or worse, leaves his skis where he threw them and departs in tears, never to return.

The problem is simply that this system, tried and sure as it is for adults, is completely inapplicable to children. Children, and especially very small children, don't learn a sport by listening. They learn by doing. Their kinetic sense is superbly educable, but only through observation and imitation. Making a child stand still in the cold can seem like punishment, and he will at the very least be bored.

Today, however, more and more ski schools have classes for children, staffed with specially trained instructors. Where such effort has been made, the results have been startling. Instructors find that children are easier to teach when the classes and the approach are designed with children in mind, children find that the business of learning to ski is a lot more fun than they expected, and parents are amazed by the progress their youngsters make.

"Rabbit Bounce" to Knee Action

by DIXI NOHL
Certified, Austrian Association of Professional Ski Instructors and U.S.
  Eastern Amateur Ski Association

The biggest problem in teaching kids to ski is getting them to do the
exercises designed to break bad habits. For instance, very young children
usually ski with absolutely stiff knees. They just don't comprehend the
command, "Bend your knees," and they won't stand still and bend them
either. A game that will cure them is to play at hopping rabbits. Let
the kids play first at hopping on the flat at the bottom of the slope, and
then coming down the slope. It's a natural and painless way to get knees
flexing. Of course, teacher must play this game with the children and hop
down the slope, too.

255

Doing the "Duck"

by KITTY HOLMES

The snowplow turn is often a confusing maneuver for a very young skier. To make turning easier and more fun, show him how to waddle like a duck on skis. Stand in a wide snowplow on flat terrain, and using an exaggerated rocking motion, shift your weight from one ski to the other. Let your child stand next to you, imitating the duck waddle on his own skis. Be certain that he learns to shift his weight between the inside edges of his skis. For sound effects and more fun, your child can quack like a duck.

When you're satisfied with your youngster's duck waddle on the flat, move up to a gradual slope. After your own demonstrations, your child can try his own snowplow turn, again rocking like a duck to shift his weight over the inside edge of the turning ski. If you practice turns in both directions, your young skier will soon learn to link his snowplow turns together.

"Pick a Flower" to Turn

by Bruce Brereton
Certified, Canadian Ski Instructors' Alliance

Young children on skis for their first or second season have difficulty understanding the movements required to steer the skis in a snowplow. For example, to make a snowplow turn to the right, a child must lean or angulate to the left and push the heel of his left ski. Often, in confusion, he will do the opposite. Terms like "angulation" and "heel thrust" will not help to relieve the child's perplexity. Instead, they make him more confused.

To get a child to do snowplow turns correctly, tell him to imagine

that a flower is growing in the snow at about the height of his knee.

As the child glides by the flower, he leans over and picks it. Then, just after he picks it, he is told to slide or push the heel of his outside ski over the snow to bury the imaginary stem and leaves of the flower. Result? The child unconsciously learns to angulate and push the heel of the ski.

The idea of a flower growing in the snow appeals to a child's imagination and sense of playing games. After two or three flower-picking turns, he will be snowplowing in perfect form.

The "Handlebar" Snowplow

by ALISON HERSEY

Certified, U.S. Eastern Amateur Ski Association

When he first attempts skiing, a youngster often lacks the physical strength to control the speed and the shape of his snowplow on lengthy ski runs. So your child can experience some fun skiing down easy trails, let him ski along between your feet until he builds up strength to maneuver on his own.

Set your skis in a wide V, pointed downhill, and place your child in the center of them. When his shorter skis are also set in a snowplow, cross one ski pole in front of his body, to serve as a handlebar. He should place his hands on the pole for easy balance and speed control in a snowplow. Encourage him to bend his knees and to lean slightly forward rather than back against your body while he skis downhill. When you think he is ready to ski on his own, lower your hands away from under the handlebar, letting him ski unaided. If he begins to tire or lose his balance, replace your hands on the poles, palms facing upward to provide support. Thus your child can learn to ski easy runs quickly, soon moving ahead to more advanced maneuvers.

Keep in Touch

by FRITZ LAVELL

A steep trail may frighten your child, and unexpectedly, he may balk at
skiing down it. You can offer a stabilizing force between your child and
the far-away bottom of the hill by assuming a normal traverse downhill
and slightly in back of him. Holding hands, traverse the trail in this
fashion. To turn, use a slow, controlled snowplow as a pivot point. Slow
down at the end of each turn before resuming a traverse below the child.
Continue skiing and holding his hand until his confidence returns. Soon
he'll be able to make the same turns on his own.

Ride 'Em T-Bar!

by KITTY HOLMES

Before your child takes his first T-bar ride, it's a good idea to brief him about the upward ascent. You can create a situation similar to riding a T-bar using your ski poles to form a T and bar.

String the shaft of one pole halfway through the strap of the other pole. Using the first pole as a T, place one side under your child's seat just at the point where a real T-bar would hit him. Standing on the other side of the T, begin walking ahead together. With your skis off, you can pull on the second pole or push on the horizontal T to illustrate how a real T-bar would feel. Do not pull too smoothly, as there will usually be a sharp jerk when your child starts his real uphill ride.

If a third person is available, you won't need to remove your skis. You and your child can sit on opposite sides of the makeshift "T" while the third party pulls the center pole shaft forward.

Hop to Parallel

by DIXI NOHL

Certified, Austrian Association of Professional Ski Instructors and U.S. Eastern Amateur Ski Association

It takes adults quite a long time to acquire enough balance, confidence, and strength to start skiing parallel. But many children have an easier time. Being naturally more limber and possessing more strength relative to their body size, they can get out of their snowplow much sooner. When a child seems confident and eager, you can usually skip some of the middle stages and push him on to parallel. When doing this, get him to hop his turn instead of snowplowing: this often results in a quick transition to parallel skiing.

The "Tired-Skier" Carry

by DIXI NOHL

Certified, Austrian Association of Professional Ski Instructors and U.S. Eastern Amateur Ski Association

Occasionally, a child who has begged his parents to take him down a run from the top of the mountain will freeze upon reaching a steep pitch or grow tired toward the end of a longer run. You can use the following method to help your child over the steep pitches or to guide him to the bottom of a trail.

1. Slip your pole straps down over the shaft of your child's poles until they rest against his pole baskets.

2. Replace your child's pole straps on his wrists so that he can grip the leather straps behind his back.

3. Grasp your pole shafts just above the baskets and spread your skis in a snowplow.

From a snowplow you can now control the speed of your child as he skis in a straight downhill running position over a steep pitch or trail. You'll find this an ideal way to negotiate troublesome terrain without frightening your young skier.

First Time on the Chair

by BOB AUTRY

Certified, Far West Ski Instructors' Association

For a beginner or a child, the first experience of riding a chairlift can be an unsettling one, and delays in loading can cause inconvenience to other skiers waiting behind in line. An experienced skier or instructor, in accompanying a novice chairlift rider, can smooth over these problems in the following way.

First, the novice should stand for a few minutes on the sidelines to watch the loading procedure and receive instruction. Then the novice and experienced skiers should step into position in the path of the approaching chair. The experienced skier should take both ski poles in one hand and gently turn the novice with his free hand either to the inside or to the outside (depending on type of chair) to align for loading. When the chair arrives, the senior places his poles across the front of the novice's body while he reaches around with the free hand and grasps the novice's parka or sweater. Gentle backward pushing with the poles and pulling on the parka will place the novice firmly in the chair.

10. CONDITIONING AND WARM-UP

Strength, to be sure, is of some importance in skiing, but it is muscular flexibility, as much as strength, that protects the skier from injury. There is an old saying in skiing that the best safety bindings are well-conditioned muscles.

Willy Schaeffler, the successful coach of Denver University and the U.S. Ski Team, puts it another way: "Don't get in condition for skiing. Get in condition for living!" It is Schaeffler's contention that there is no need for dull, laborious "living room" fitness programs in October if you hike, swim, water ski, row, fence, or play handball in summer or take a brisk half-hour walk every day when that isn't possible. It should be recognized that muscles *must work* to stay in shape. It does not matter whether this work is in the form of play or calisthenics. Its rewards are more than worthwhile: better skiing and a strong sense of well-being.

"V for Victory"

by WILLY SCHAEFFLER

A boy who wants to ski four ways for Denver University (slalom, downhill, cross-country, and jumping) has to perform as many as two hundred different exercises during his fall conditioning. One exercise that's used by all our skiers is a belly conditioner that the boys affectionately call "V for victory."

Getting your midsection in shape will definitely help your skiing this winter. For instance, you could have a well-coordinated set of arms and shoulders and well-coordinated legs, but you have to put the two together to ski well. That means strong stomach muscles and strong muscles in the small of your back. "V for victory" will build these muscles for you.

From a lying-down position, simultaneously lift your shoulders and legs off the ground, balancing on your buttocks. In this position, begin to move your torso and legs in all directions with legs extended. Exercise in this V position for fifteen seconds to start. In succeeding exercise sessions, build up your endurance until you can go for thirty seconds. When you get out on the slopes, your midsection will be in the right shape to work your whole body in the turn.

268

Be a Stationary Slalom Racer

by WILLY SCHAEFFLER

Try the "stationary slalom" used by the Denver University ski team. From a standing position, begin to jump your feet from one direction to the other, pretending that you are skiing through a slalom flush or a series of tightly set gates going directly down the hill. To vary the exercise, imagine that the racecourse now opens up into a series of long turns: now jump higher and farther from side to side. Then revert back to short hops. Start out by doing this exercise for half a minute, simply do it until you run out of wind. Keep increasing each day. Pretty soon your legs and lungs will be in shape to take you down the equivalent of a whole mountain.

Down by the Up Staircase

by JACK G. BRINER

In making a series of short turns down the fall line, many skiers have a problem in coming up and forward for rhythmic unweighting of the skis. If you experience this difficulty in your skiing, it may be partly due to your lack of coordination, and it may be partly due to softness in the muscles you need for this kind of skiing.

To learn the rhythmic coordination required for short swing skiing and to get the requisite leg muscles in shape before the season starts, try the following exercise. Stand in a traverse position at the bottom of a staircase and assume that up the stairs is the equivalent of down the fall line. Now, hop up one stair, twisting your feet into a new traverse position. Repeat hopping up succeeding stairs, twisting your feet under you while keeping your shoulders steady. About eight stairs is enough to establish the rhythm.

Repeat the exercise daily, increasing the number of stairs you "ski down." It will quickly condition your leg muscles, teach you the coordination needed to unweight up and forward, and will establish the rhythm you must have to handle short swings on steep slopes.

Pre-Strengthen Your Legs

by HENRY WITTENBERG

Everyone should make some attempt before the ski season to strengthen his leg muscles. Strong muscles and joints not only will enable you to start off skiing better, but they will add to your safety by resisting injury.

Many skiers find isometric or resistance exercises, when used as a supplement to regular isotonic exercising, a quick and convenient way to build up strength. One exercise that is particularly valuable is called the "leg extensor." To do it, find a piece of rope about forty inches long and tie it in a loop. Sit on a chair and place the loop around your ankles. Inhale deeply and hold your breath. Force your right leg forward, keeping your left foot flat on the floor. Increase the exertion in your right leg for four seconds. Now hold this effort at a maximum for six seconds. Relax and exhale. Repeat this ten-second isometric exercise with the left leg. Perform it only once during any exercise session. Along with your other exercises, you should start this one about five weeks before the ski season starts. Your legs will be in great shape by the time you hit the slopes.

Ankle-Strengthening Exercises

by BILLY KIDD

Ankle-strengthening exercises can be done without leaving your chair (providing a constructive way to elude the passivity of TV watching, while you're at it).

Simply move your foot in a certain direction while applying resistance with your hand. For instance, press your hand down on the top of your

foot and twist your foot up to stretch the top muscles; pull your foot back, then press forward against your hands. An alternate: pull your foot up with your hand, then twist your foot down, resisting with your hand (as shown on page 273). Building ankles in this way will loosen ligaments, giving you limber, flexible ankle joints that will be more sprain proof. These exercises will also make turning and stem maneuvers easier and give you greater edge control.

Another good trick is as follows: Place a book that is two to two and a half inches thick on the floor, and with your toes and part of the soles of your feet on the book, lift yourself up and balance on the edge. Repeat this until you feel your calves burning. It will strengthen your feet, ankles, and calf muscles and will help you improve your balance.

The Tune-Up Trunk Twist

by H. H. MERRIFIELD

One way to ensure a better first run of the day is to get your body moving before you set off down the slope. It will not only warm you up after a long lift ride, but it will loosen and relax your muscles.

To increase the flexibility of your shoulders and trunk, try a twisting motion. Stand with your feet together and put your poles behind your back with an elbow grip. Now bend forward at the waist and rotate your body until your poles point toward your skis. Repeat this rotating in both directions until you feel limber.